WOMEN
HISTORY, IDENTITY & INFLUENCE

WOMEN HISTORY, IDENTITY & INFLUENCE

JULIA C. MORRIS

SIRIUS

SIRIUS

This edition published in 2022 by Sirius Publishing, a division of
Arcturus Publishing Limited,
26/27 Bickels Yard, 151–153 Bermondsey Street,
London SE1 3HA

ISBN: 978-1-3988-2078-4
AD007309UK

Printed in Singapore

Contents

Introduction

Amanda Gorman, America's first National Youth Poet Laureate, and the youngest inaugural poet ever, emerged as one of the most inspiring young artists of the female renaissance when she read her poem 'The Hill We Climb' at President Joe Biden and Vice President Kamala Harris's 2021 inauguration. Describing her background as 'a skinny Black girl, descended from slaves and raised by a single mother', who 'can dream of becoming president only to find herself reciting for one', Gorman powerfully voiced intersecting issues of feminism and marginalization. In many Western cultures, long-standing practices of domination and control have all too often seen the voices of women – and Black women in particular – sidelined in favour of men.

Just looking at the statistics reveals the contemporary contours of women's struggles still commonplace worldwide. The latest United Nations *World's Women* report shows that 60 per cent of the world's poorest people are women and girls. More than half of all children unable to attend school are girls. Women's representation in parliament has doubled globally; however, women still only hold 25 per cent of parliamentary seats. Among Fortune 500 corporations, only 7.4 per cent, or 37 chief executive officers, are women. Women are also disproportionately affected by health-related concerns, intimate partner violence and environmental degradation, since access to resources is so

Amanda Gorman speaking at the 2021 presidential inauguration in Washington, DC.

often stratified by gender in violent and painful ways. Yet these gender disparities are not going unnoticed. Prevailing gender norms are being challenged in inspiring ways through the trailblazing efforts of female, male and non-gender-binary feminists alike.

Women have long exerted influential sway around the world, providing the bedrock that has led figures like Amanda Gorman to rise so prominently on the global scene. In fact, in some cultures around the world, known as matriarchal societies, women have traditonally commanded the power and authority. In other cultural contexts, conceptions of gender identity have not adhered to two discrete categories of 'female' and 'male' as thought of in many Western societies. Indeed, gender roles and appearance look staggeringly different around the world and at different periods over time, reflecting prevalent contemporary social norms and thinking. Although humans are born with biological sex, we learn to be women and men through culturally specific practices and institutions. As soon as we are born, we start to learn how to talk, walk, dress, eat, think and express our emotions in gendered ways. We learn what kinds of behaviour are perceived as masculine or feminine and what we 'should' or 'should not' do. Looking at differing conceptions of gender identity through a cultural comparative and historical lens shows us how gender is culturally constructed through institutional practices in education, family attitudes, religion, media and the state. This recognition that 'innate' superiority on the basis of gender is not 'inevitable' or 'natural' further animates our understandings that 'being a woman' should not limit one's realm of possibilities.

Gender – and perceived biological differences between 'woman' and 'man' – has long been used as a mechanism of control. Just glancing at the historical figures still upheld in textbooks, museums, the media and other institutions, we get a limited sense of the prominence of women throughout global history. Women have long been written out of the record of certain fields, such as in science, technology, engineering and mathematics (STEM) professions, despite their pioneering roles. Historiography is overwhelmingly white, male dominated and often legitimized by myths going back to the 'man the hunter, woman the gatherer' trope, whereby women are depicted as passive members of the group. However, no known historical or contemporary foraging societies or primate groups display the division of labour of the hunter-gatherer stereotype. This fairytale has only served to reinforce the idea that men and women have some essentially different nature that was shaped in our primordial past. In reality, since the dawn of humanity, women have changed the world as incredible leaders, warriors, athletes, innovators, reformers, advocates, activists and scholars. Women have ruled empires, traversed the skies, fronted political and social movements, produced prolific literature, art and music, and pioneered ground-breaking inventions and discoveries.

This book explores many different cultural systems and historical eras in order to recognize the influential role that women have played in challenging and resisting gender stereotypes and inequalities through creative strategies. Certainly, many men have also been important figures in advancing the rights of women and upending female subordination. However, centring female voices enables us to celebrate women who have long challenged the status quo but been marginalized from view. Gender-specific histories are important because they allow for the recognition that while gender is a social construct, there *are* specific inequalities related to gender divisions. Women are not valued equally, and disproportionately suffer in regions around the world. Failing to foreground women's lives would mean pretending that women have not been excluded for centuries, and to do so would naturalize systems of sex and gender discrimination.

The story of women's history, identity and influence is a record of dynamism, brilliant creativity and determination where women of all backgrounds have dreamed big and broken barriers. The triumphs and challenges evident in the amazing achievements and legacies of these heroes past and present provide the foundations for the heroes of today.

Chapter

1 WOMEN IN ANTIQUITY

OUR VISION TODAY OF THE PALAEOLITHIC ERA or Stone Age, which lasted from roughly three million years ago until 10,0000BCE, is dominated by cartoons and museum dioramas of fur-clad macho male hunters, but the reality was quite different. In fact, there has never been one single way that early *homo sapiens* organized social life by sex. As humans developed complex civilizations, such as the ancient Egyptians, Greeks and Maya, there emerged all manner of gender diversity that contributed to social life and to our development as humans.

A bust of the ancient Egyptian queen, Nefertiti, who reigned from 1353–1336BCE.

Woman the gatherer?

From the familiar story of 'man the hunter, woman the gatherer' to the Christian biblical tale of the fallen Eve, created after and from Adam, Western mythologies have typically cast women in passive, inferior or heretical roles. In Western historical accounts of early humans, human males are depicted as fierce, dominant hunters because of their supposed genetically gifted strength and cunning. As the story goes, men – like the great primates from which they descended – ruled the savannahs, plains and jungles. Using their mighty strength, they hunted to sustain themselves, their tribe, their sexual partners and their offspring. Hunting demanded aggression, ingenuity, dominance, male bonding and long periods away from the home. This stereotype of primal male dominance is often referred to as an argument that masculine behaviour is somehow genetically imprinted on human DNA or hardwired into the human brain.

According to this line of thought, man is predisposed to derive pleasure from killing animals, a notion that still shapes the human male psyche for violence and aggression to this day. Women, by contrast, supposedly had a much gentler disposition and naturally assumed the role of gatherers, waiting patiently at home for men to bring the meat. They collected nuts, fruits and seeds, and were more sedentary, domestically oriented, child focused, nurturing, social and passive. Allegedly, contemporary gender roles of 'man the breadwinner' and 'woman the caregiver', along with hierarchies of power, rights and resources, emerged from physical or mental behavioural differences that matured during human evolution. To this day, we still see the Tarzan and Jane stereotype used time and again in films, cartoons, consumer goods and even some popular and scientific writing.

The Celtic queen Boudica ruled the East Anglian Iceni tribe of Great Britain. A freedom fighter, she led a vast uprising against oppressive Roman rule in 60CE.

Popular representations of early human gender roles are epitomized by the club-carrying caveman who drags off 'his woman' by her hair.

This narrative of human origins is closely associated with evolutionary psychology and is often invoked to explain the 'naturalness' of contemporary differences in gender roles. In reality, the hunter-gatherer myth was developed by early-20th-century anthropologists, the field being dominated at that time by white Euro-American male researchers. Steeped in Western behavioural stereotypes, their findings and analyses were shaped by the gender-biased lens that they applied. However, recent archaeological evidence and anthropological research has pushed back against this scenario. Countless examples exist of hunter-gatherer societies in earlier eras – and to this day – in which female hunters dominate. Human remains have been found around the world of women buried with arrows, spears, battle-axes and swords used in big-game hunting. These findings dispute the hypothesis that hunting is incompatible with maternal responsibilities or that all women had children or assumed caregiving roles in the first place. An egalitarian and highly flexible division of labour makes good evolutionary sense. Everyone could be trained in a wide range of skill sets to contribute to the group's collective flourishing when changing circumstances arose. Regardless, all tasks were equally crucial to the collective success of human groups, whether that be through foraging, hunting, providing logistical support, fabricating clothing, weaponry and transportation or tending to the well-being of the young and old.

Excavations at the Wilamaya Patjxa site in Peru unearthed a 9,000-year-old female skeleton buried with what archaeologists call a 'big-game-hunting kit'. Additional research led the archaeologists to conclude that early females in the Americas were big-game hunters. There was close to equal participation in hunting for the sexes, demonstrating that in this region, gender roles were highly fluid.

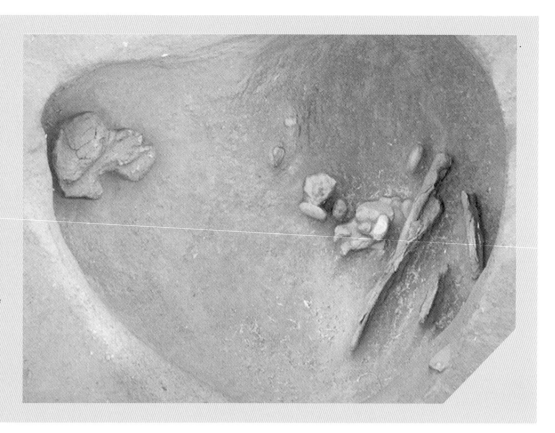

Among the Agta Negrito people of the Philippines, women and men actively participate in hunting, both singly and together. They spear fish and hunt wild pig and deer using bows and arrows, knives and dogs.

Anthropologists have also recently pushed backed against popular theories surrounding the importance of hunting to hunter-gatherer societies. Food foraging was the primary survival strategy of our ancestors before the introduction of agriculture. Hunting was simply not the universal foundational activity of early human groups. Fossil evidence shows that the teeth of Palaeolithic humans were adapted to an omnivorous diet comprised principally of plants and seeds, bulked up by meat only when it was available. Humans were in fact more likely to be a prey species and survived through scavenging rather than hunting. Many of our modern human characteristics, such as socialization and co-operation, probably developed from this fact of being a prey species and our ability to outsmart predators. Key to our development was our cognitive growth compared to other animals. Our larger brains require the consumption of 'brain foods' from selective nutrients found in edible plants, small animals, eggs, insects and shellfish, not meat from game. So, although earlier hypotheses uphold big-game hunting and meat eating as male-dominated activities that brought about our evolutionary superiority over generations, in reality, foraging played a greater role in developing crucial biological and behavioural traits that distinguish humans from other primates.

*Running horned woman from 6,000–4,000*BCE, *pigment on rock, Tassili n'Ajjer, Algeria.*

LEFT: *Pueblo ceremonial shield warrior carved on Comanche Gap volcanic dyke in Galisteo Basin Preserve, New Mexico, USA, 1325–1680CE.*

RIGHT: *Coal drawing illustrating women as key participants in hunting, Dinwoody tradition rock art, Wyoming, USA.*

WHO AUTHORS OUR PREHISTORIC PAST?

The incumbent of the tomb of a great Viking warrior in Birka, Sweden was assumed to be male by archaeologists in the late 1800s. The 10th-century chamber grave was filled with weaponry, horses and a game board thought to be for mapping out military strategies. Using genomic sequencing, archaeologists discovered in 2017 that the high-ranking warrior was in fact biologically female. This finding, and others from the archaeological record, provoked a great deal of debate about how modern ideas of gender roles affect historical interpretations and make it difficult to create universal assumptions of gender divisions across both prehistoric and later humans.

In some of those societies where the division of labour falls along 'man-hunter/woman-gatherer' lines, there is no status associated with hunting versus gathering. The Batek people in Malaysia, for example, are generally taken to be one of the most egalitarian societies in the world. Hunting and plant knowledge both have great cultural significance. The Batek see themselves as a collective and interdependent group, in which all people make important contributions towards the community as a whole. They have no rigid rules separating gender roles. Women can and do hunt if they choose, as well as occupying chieftains' roles.

Goddesses who rule

'I am Beyoncé Giselle Knowles-Carter,' sings Beyoncé in 'Mood 4 Eva', a track on her 2020 visual album *Black Is King*. 'I am the Nala, sister of Naruba, Osun, Queen Sheba, I am the mother.' Beyoncé has positioned herself with different goddesses throughout her music career, incorporating into her performances iconography from across the world's religious traditions. From evoking Osun (the West African Yoruba goddess of love, sensuality and femininity) and Kali (the Hindu goddess of time, creation and destruction) to making a splash with her Instagram maternity announcement, in which she merged the Catholic Virgin Mary and Roman goddess Venus, Beyoncé has long adopted goddess archetypes as feminist symbols of strength and power. She is not alone. Other mainstream music artists have also reworked goddess imagery to make important statements about femininity and gender inequality. In 2018, for instance, Ariana Grande turned heads and met with feminist critical acclaim when she released the music video to her song 'God is a Woman', in which she straddles a globe.

This is nothing new. Beyoncé and other prominent cultural icons are drawing on a rich history of goddess worship. Human history is filled with fierce mythological women who are revered to this day, dating back to the earliest records we have of human civilization. As warriors, mothers, magicians and lovers, female goddesses are of crucial importance across the world's religious traditions and in the ancient cultures of Mesopotamia, Greece and Egypt. They hold powerful capabilities such as divine prophecy, healing, protection, love, fertility and wisdom.

Theories about goddess worship have long been advanced by social scientists. Some specialists in comparative religion and human psychology suggest that goddess worship is connected with theories of social development. The 19th-century Swiss historian J.J. Bachofen (1815–87) argued that early human societies were matriarchal, something that was reflected in female deity worship. The Austrian psychoanalyst Sigmund Freud (1856–1939) also believed that goddess worship was connected to earlier human stages of matriarchy, before later periods of patriarchy. In her book *When God Was a Woman* (1976), the feminist researcher Merlin Stone (1931–2011) argued that female religion flourished for thousands of years but was violently suppressed in the Middle East by new patriarchal Judaeo-Christian cultures.

Today, many feminist scholars of comparative religions reject this. They argue instead that most prominent goddesses were born in ancient patriarchal societies. For example, the ancient Greeks may have worshipped goddesses, but real-life women had few rights in comparison to male citizens. There is a danger in glossing over these systems of oppression or how many religions solidified patriarchal control through appeals to the supernatural. In other words, the symbolism of

Matriarchy versus patriarchy – in matriarchal societies, women hold overall power, whereas patriarchal societies are the reverse.

Gynaecocracy – government by women or a state in which women hold supreme command.

Beyoncé and other mainstream music artists such as Nicki Minaj, Ariana Grande and Madonna have used goddess imagery and narratives to push back against assumptions around gender, race and motherhood. By reappropriating Virgin Mary iconography, Beyoncé challenges the idea that whiteness equals purity and that motherhood cannot be compatible with sexuality. At the same time, however, some feminist critics have charged that these glamorized images do not radically challenge conventional sexist constructions of female identity. What do you think?

goddess worship cannot straightforwardly depict gender relationships in societies. Sometimes deities might reflect the reality of social roles, but more often they could also represent alternative concepts of community or connect to complex psychic impulses. Nevertheless, the prominence of female goddesses across the world's religions powerfully shows the influence that women have commanded throughout the ages in different shapes and forms.

The oldest records we have of human civilization date back to the ancient Mesopotamian civilization of Sumer, which existed from the fifth to the third millennium BCE. Often referred to as 'the cradle of civilization', Sumer sprawled along the Fertile Crescent between the Tigris and Euphrates rivers in what is present-day Iraq and Kuwait. Sumerians were some of the first people to develop agriculture on a grand scale, driven by their invention of the plough and irrigation canals. They also had tremendous cultural achievements in writing, language, architecture, mathematics, law, religion and astronomy. The Sumerian language is used in the oldest known linguistic records, appearing in archaeological finds dated to around 3100BCE. Its script, cuneiform, is one of the earliest systems of writing.

Sumerian religion was polytheistic, meaning that they worshipped multiple gods, many of whom were anthropomorphic, taking a human-like form. The Sumerian

INANNA, THE GODDESS OF 'THE FEARSOME POWERS'

One of the most revered Sumerian goddesses was Inanna, the goddess of love and war. She was widely honoured for embodying love, sensuality, fertility, courage and war. She is mentioned across Mesopotamian mythologies, including in the legendary *Epic of Gilgamesh* – the world's earliest surviving notable literature. Inanna was the patron deity of the great city of Uruk, although she had temples across most cities. She is often depicted in battledress in the company of lions, showing her courage and supremacy. She was described as an independent goddess who did as she pleased, sometimes to the extreme! Later known as Ishtar among the Assyrians, Inanna inspired similar deities in other cultures, including the Greek Athena and the Roman Minerva.

pantheon of goddesses and gods brims with prominent female deities. Temples to these deities were built atop vast ziggurats, which were at the heart of all major Sumerian city-states. These impressive tiered, pyramid-like temples reached skyward – some attained a height of nearly 91 m (300 ft) – and were places to summon divine intervention. The Sumerians believed that their gods lived in the sky, so to be heard by them required being as high as possible. Each Sumerian city had a principal god to whom the temple was dedicated. Major female deities were revered for their divine powers. They included Nanshe (the goddess of social justice and prophecy), Ninhursag (the Sumerian mother goddess), Nidaba (the goddess of writing, learning and the harvest) and Ninkasi (the celebrated goddess of alcohol).

Goddesses such as Tiamat (*see* box) feature heavily in the creation myths of many of the world's religions. Although most Western societies are now embedded in patriarchal religions and customs, Ariana Grande's assertion that 'God is a Woman' should not be surprising. Archaeological evidence suggests that God was taken to be female in many contexts, with early Christian writings and texts referring to God in feminine terms. At other times, God transcends socially constructed notions of gender in Christian texts. In the Hebrew Bible, for example, God's personal name, Yahweh, which is revealed to Moses, combines both female and male grammatical endings. It was only after the 10th century that depictions of God as an elderly white man began to surface in Western art, and thereby helped solidify gender and racial inequality. Yet theologians argue that attempting to pinpoint the reality of God blocks religious experiences. God is simply 'being' and cannot be anthropomorphized in this way.

Long before the major world religions were established, many of our early human ancestors venerated a supreme female creator in their belief systems. Representations of a mother goddess have surfaced globally, demonstrating that goddess worship played a central role in the emergence of virtually every prominent civilization.

Women were not just prominent in religious and ritual realms. The Sumerians also had a powerful female monarch, Kubaba, who ruled the city-state of Kish around 2500BCE. Archaeologists discovered the 'King List', a Sumerian clay tablet that documents the ancient rulers of Sumer. Within this text, Kubaba is documented as making 'firm the foundations of Kish' and advancing a dynasty that lasted 100 years.

Tiamat was the goddess of the salt sea and primordial chaos in the religion of ancient Babylon (1895–539BCE) – the civilization established by the Akkadians, who eventually took over the land of the Sumerians. In the Babylonian epic of creation, *Enūma Elish*, Tiamat gives birth to the first generation of gods through a sacred marriage between the sweet and salt waters. Tiamat is eventually defeated by the storm god Marduk, the patron deity of Babylon, who forms the earth and heavens from her divided body. She is depicted as a female serpent or dragon who gives birth to a variety of monsters, including scorpion men and mer-people.

The Creation of God, Harmonia Rosales, 2017.

Establishing counter-narratives

In her painting *The Creation of God* (2017), the Afro-Cuban American artist Harmonia Rosales reinterprets Michelangelo's *The Creation of Adam* from the Sistine Chapel in Vatican City. Rosales paints God as a Black woman, creating life in Her own image, to flip the script on white men as central figures of authority.

Challenging assumptions: the Venus of Hohle Fels

The figurine of the Venus of Hohle Fels, discovered in south-western Germany, is the oldest piece of figurative art and also the earliest image of a human being ever to be found. It is made of mammoth ivory and dates from the Palaeolithic period, between 40,000 and 35,000 years ago. It measures just under 6 cm (2.4 in), but with proportionally large breasts, belly, thighs and genitalia. Several hypotheses have been advanced about the figurine, the most prominent being that it is a fertility goddess, representing abundance during the extremely challenging period of the late

Ice Age. Its existence suggests that early humans developed a belief system that involved the concept of a deity personified as female. This is backed up by the fact that similar statuettes and wall engravings have been found throughout the region.

Three views of the Venus of Hohle Fels.

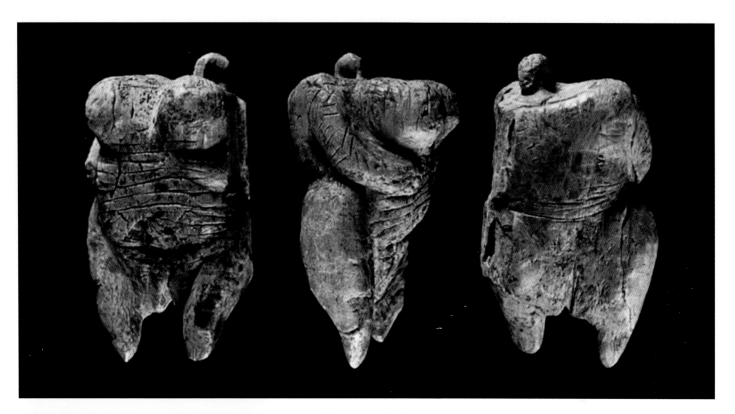

Mother goddess or ancient selfie?

Together with Mesopotamia and ancient Egypt, the Indus Valley Civilization (also known as the Harappan Civilization) was the earliest civilization of the Near East and South Asia. Lasting from 3300 to 1300BCE, it was also the most widespread, spanning north-east Afghanistan, the majority of Pakistan and western India. Harappan cities were renowned for their efficient urban planning, elaborate water supply and drainage systems, and advanced techniques in handicrafts. Archaeological excavations have unearthed a number of early terracotta statuettes of female forms. Differing hypotheses suggest that these are representations of a mother goddess or even self-portraits of their makers. Regardless, historians believe this to be an egalitarian period, during which women held an important place in Harappan society and possibly wielded great power.

Mother goddess from the Indus Valley Civilization.

AN ICON OF FEMINISM?

Worship of Kali dates to the first millennium BCE. Kali is a fierce manifestation of the great Hindu mother goddess Devi. It is widely understood that Devi's many contrasting aspects embody the existential freedom to be, whereby the feminine has all manner of complex sides and gender is not a limiting condition.

In contrast to the patriarchal god of contemporary Judaeo-Christian traditions, Hinduism has a pantheon of powerful female goddesses. Many argue that the widespread acceptance and valorization of goddess figures in Hinduism provides models of women that push back against submissive gender stereotypes in Hindu folkloric texts, such as the *Ramayana* (c.500–100BCE). The recognition of women's spiritual power has also supported the rise of women political leaders such as Indira Gandhi. But while goddesses are revered in much of Indian culture, it is often men who have ultimate authority in Indian society. This is reflected in terms of female life expectancy, literacy, income, subjection to violence and equality of opportunity.

Images of Hindu goddesses and their power or *shakti* have been heavily utilized in recent years by political and women's rights campaigns. The 'Abused Goddesses' campaign shown here employs Hindu goddesses to address gender-based violence, depicting an image of Durga, the all-powerful mother goddess, with bruises and black eyes. The campaign received global attention for making visible the contradictions of female deification and oppression. However, critics charge that these portrayals focus on illustrating women as passive victims. Furthermore, they are all represented as light-skinned, upper-caste Brahmin Hindu women. This, they argue, marginalizes dark-skinned Indian women and those from lower castes and classes.

The mother goddess

In Indian Hinduism, Devi is the great mother goddess, celebrated extensively across ancient Indian literature and in the iconography of Hindu temples around the world. Devi takes thousands of forms, including as Durga the warrior and protector goddess, who rides a ferocious tiger as she charges into battle to destroy evil. Another form is Kali, the creator and destroyer goddess. Kali is depicted with a blood-soaked sword that she uses to cut the bonds of ego and ignorance, which are also represented by the severed demon head held in one of her many hands. Alongside this, Kali is Mother Nature, representing the time prior to the existence of this world.

Despite the prominence of female goddesses around the world, including as personified deifications of creation, many goddess-worshipping civilizations had receded by 1500BCE. In their place arose monotheistic religions that cemented the worship of male-centred orders that revolve around a patriarchal leadership of God, father, king and priest. These masculine-geared theologies placed the goddess in a subordinate status, often with a man as her dominant husband, and no longer as the supreme female deity from which everything emerged. In Europe and under the Crusades and colonialism, many allegedly 'pagan' religions that venerated powerful female deities were suppressed by Christian emperors and, during the Middle Ages, by centuries of witch hunts. To this day, it remains hotly debated whether male-dominated religions displaced prehistoric matriarchal orders. Nevertheless, in recent years, goddess cults have resurged, worshipped by the modern-day Wicca movement and Neopaganism.

MODERN-DAY WORSHIP

Wicca is a contemporary spiritual and nature-focused movement that revives ancient indigenous, pre-Christian goddess beliefs from around the world. Wiccans worship nature, often personified as Mother Earth and Father Sky. With the rise of feminism, new Neopagan traditions have centred goddess worship around composites of feminine deities from past and present world cultures. Gaia, the primordial Greek deity of all life and the personification of Earth, often features.

FIERCE FEMALE DEITIES

Mami Wata is the great water deity venerated across West, Central and Southern Africa, as well as in the African diaspora. Often represented as a mermaid or snake charmer, she is honoured as the sacred nature of water who can bring good or bad fortune depending on how well she is appeased.

Amaterasu is the great celestial sun goddess of the Japanese Shinto religion. She is represented in Japan's earliest texts from c.700CE as the ruler of the Plain of High Heaven or Takamagahara. To this day, the Grand Shrine of Ise is one of Shinto's holiest sites and Amaterasu's chief place of worship.

Pele is the fierce goddess of volcanoes and fire in ancient Hawaiian mythology, who both destroys and creates land. Pele was the principal deity prior to the US annexation of Hawaii and is still venerated, despite missionary attempts to suppress traditional religious beliefs.

Venerated as the 'mother of gods and mortals', Coatlicue or 'Serpent Skirt' was the major Aztec earth goddess who gave birth to the moon, stars and Huitzilopochtli, the god of sun and war. Coatlicue is depicted as a woman with a face of two serpents confronting each other. She wears a skirt of writhing snakes and a necklace of human hearts, hands and a skull, and has claws for fingers and toes.

The powerful women of ancient Egypt

The ancient Egyptian civilization dates from the time of the unification of Upper and Lower Egypt in 3000BCE – known as the First Dynasty – to eventual conquest by the Greeks under Alexander the Great in 332BCE.

For close to 30 centuries, Egypt was the leading civilization of the Mediterranean world. As rulers, major commercial players, scientists, engineers, physicians, priests and more, women played a crucial part in advancing its dominant rule. Unlike many other ancient cultures dominated by patriarchal norms, in ancient Egypt women occupied a prominent social position and were equal to men under the law. They held positions of power and worked in the public sphere at all levels of society, including commanding vast commercial enterprises and owning property. That this was unique, at least in the Mediterranean region at that time, is reflected in the surviving accounts we have of this period. The Greek historian Herodotus was shocked at the gender egalitarianism in Egypt. Writing in the fifth century BCE, he described the role of Egyptian women as having seemingly 'reversed the ordinary practices of mankind…. Women attend market and are employed in trade, while men stay at home and do the weaving.' Clearly, Herodotus was coming from a particular mindset: he used the gendered term 'mankind', whereas the Egyptians used the inclusive gender-neutral 'humankind'!

EARLY STEM PIONEERS

Gender egalitarianism in professions was not commonplace across many ancient cultures. However, the situation in ancient Egypt was quite different. The ancient Egyptians had an advanced medical system, in which female medical specialists played important roles. Peseshet, who lived under the Fourth Dynasty (c.2613–2484BCE), is often credited as the world's earliest known female physician.

Egyptians understood the universe to be a duality of female and male. The female deity, Maat, symbolized this cosmic harmony that applied to the egalitarianism of gender roles. The earliest creation myths emphasize the importance of women and men as cohesive complements to one another. Maat was seen as personifying truth, justice and cosmic order.

Maat is often depicted in paintings with wings or an ostrich feather on her head. In mortuary rituals, she weighed the heart of the deceased person's soul in the scales of justice. Her spirit of harmony and balance – the principle of maat – lay at the heart of Egyptian moral codes and was said to be spread over the Earth.

THE RIGHTS OF WOMEN IN ANCIENT EGYPT

- Occupy all positions, including as pharaohs, governors, judges and prime ministers

- Receive payments for commercial transactions

- Own and inherit property independently

- Buy and sell land

- Pay taxes

- Freely choose a partner

- Adopt children in one's own name

- Make legal challenges and settlements, such as marriage, separation and inheritance

- Travel

- Drink alcohol

- Religious egalitarianism

NB: it is difficult to make generalizations without taking into consideration other factors such as status, ethnicity, class, wealth and age. Many of these rights were more accessible for women of higher classes.

The mighty Hatshepsut reigned supreme c.1473–1458BCE. Her rule was a time of great prosperity, filled with incredible building projects, the expansion of trade and magnificent art.

Equal opportunity

Women were high priestesses to gods and goddesses in ancient Egypt, holding similar positions to their male counterparts and receiving the same pay. By comparison, consider some of the equal opportunity that women struggle to achieve today!

Literacy and education

Sesaht or 'female scribe' was the Egyptian goddess of writing. But the role of women as writers was not confined to the spiritual realm. In fact, in ancient Egypt, the education of girls was common. Women from higher classes were often literate and could hold the highly valued position of scribe: writing up contracts, taking censuses and performing all manner of important administrative transcriptions.

Women high priestesses in ancient Egypt.

A *carving of Sesaht holding a stylus, used for engraving.*

Women in positions of power

Ancient Egypt is well known for its powerful female rulers. Although the majority of the rulers of ancient Egypt were men, a number of powerful queens, five of whom became pharaohs in their own rights, held sway over the empire. In fact, the ancient Egyptian empire saw more women in positions of power than any other culture in the ancient world – and arguably many in the present! However, many of these successful female rulers' legacies were completely erased after their death or made into sensationalized stories to justify patriarchal rule and the subjugation of women in positions of power.

The status of women declined in Egypt after Roman annexation in 30BCE and then especially under the Byzantine empire in the fourth century CE. Under this regime, Christianity rose to prominence, bringing with it limiting beliefs about women as connected to biblical mythology. The Muslim conquest of Egypt between 639 and 646CE was the final nail in the coffin of the gender equality that had existed for almost 3,000 years.

DANCERS, ACROBATS AND JUGGLERS

Music, singing and dancing were important parts of life in ancient Egypt. Professional female entertainers were often venerated and would perform at parties, banquets, royal celebrations and religious temples. Music schools for women existed in ancient Egypt, where girls from high-ranking familities typically received specialized training. The highest status of temple musician – the office of 'musician' (*shemayet*) – was frequently held by women. However, women acted as entertainers across the social scale.

FROM FIERCE TO FELINE

Bastet was a fierce lioness warrior goddess of the sun who had a hugely popular cult following across the Mediterranean world. The lion-like qualities of royal women were emphasized by the wearing of feline claw amulets. Hatshepsut was often represented as a lion-like sphinx when she ruled. Bastet was orginally depicted as a lioness. Her symbolization as a cat reflects subtle changes in gender beliefs, aligning women with gentler, 'less threatening' species.

Cleopatra VII

The legendary Cleopatra VII (69–30BCE) was the last active pharaoh in Ptolemaic Egypt. She ruled Egypt for 21 years and, at the height of her power, controlled almost the entirety of the eastern Mediterranean coast: the final great kingdom of any Egyptian ruler. She married her brother, Ptolemy XIII, by her father's orders. However, she made it clear that she would not share power with him and had his name removed from official documents. His face was also kept off all currency: an honour reserved for herself alone! She was highly educated, was known to speak nine languages, commanded an army and navy, regulated the economy and justice system, and negotiated expertly with foreign powers, including the advancing Roman Empire. Her reign was filled with stories of intrigue, including her affairs with the Emperor Julius Ceasar and Caesar's protégé Mark Antony. It is no wonder that she remains so ubiquitous in popular culture: from films, plays and music to even an asteroid named after her, 216 Kleopatra!

Statue of a Ptolemaic queen holding a cornucopia or horn of plenty, sometimes identified as Cleopatra VII. Her hairstyle and dress suggest a date in the second or first century BCE. The cartouche reading 'Cleopatra' on her arm is not correctly oriented, so is probably a modern addition.

Navigating patriarchal control in ancient Greece

The ancient Greek civilization was a collection of city-states that flourished from c.800BCE until domination by the Roman Empire in 146BCE

The ancient Greek civilization prospered at a similar time to Egypt but could not have been more different in terms of the rights accorded women. Unlike in other civilizations in the ancient world, Greek women were considered second-class citizens. They could not vote, own land or inherit, and lived under a patriarchal ideology that they be confined to the home to rear children and support their husband. From birth to death, Greek women lived under the control of a guardian or *kyrios*. Generally, this would be their father then later their husband or another relative. The extent of the *kyrios*'s power depended on a woman's status and where they lived in Greece. However, the *kyrios* usually had control over whom a woman married and all economic transactions she made over a certain value. The Greek statesman and general Pericles characterized the misogynistic attitudes of the time, stating that: 'The greatest glory of a woman is to be least talked about, whether they are praising you or criticizing you!'

DOMINATION AND TACTICAL RESISTANCE

Women sometimes dressed as men to navigate the systems of control imposed on them. This was the case with the Greek physician Agnodice of Athens, whose challenges to the male-dominated profession shifted the laws on women practising medicine. At the time, women could not practise medicine under penalty of death. Denied a medical education in Athens, Agnodice travelled to Egypt to study and then returned to Athens disguised as a man to practise. She became so popular that she was accused of seducing her female patients by rival male doctors. During her trial she revealed that she was a woman and was threatened with execution. She was saved by a group of prominent Athenian women, who managed to advocate for her acquittal. After her trial, the laws were changed, enabling women to practise medicine on a more equal footing with men.

Despite the overwhelming suppression experienced by women in ancient Greece, a number of women escaped the limitations of Greek society and achieved lasting acclaim. These women were from elite families. Many women across ancient Greece would not have had their lives and deeds recorded.

Sappho of Lesbos (620–570BCE)

The female teacher and poet Sappho of Lesbos (620–570BCE) was famed for the intense passion of her poetry. Known as the 'Tenth Music' and 'The Poetess', she was an influential figure in the local community on the island of Lesbos, where she attracted a group of literary female students at her academy for unmarried young women. Sappho is most famous for the unique metrical form of her poetry. Even today, the 'Sapphic stanza' refers to a verse form of four-line stanzas. Sappho's work attracted critical acclaim among Greek and Roman poets and is still well known to this day. However, her incredible legacy was long obscured by discussions of her sexuality and her 'moral reputation' as a woman. Think how women in power still face these kinds of objectifying criticisms over their identity and appearance that devalue their ideas.

A bust of Sappho of Lesbos held at the Capitoline Museum in Rome.

Queen Gorgo of Sparta (518–508BCE)

Queen Gorgo of Sparta (518–508BCE) was queen of the Greek city-state of ancient Sparta, known for her great wisdom and authority in a heavily male-dominated world. Women in Sparta had a higher degree of freedom than elsewhere in ancient Greece. Gorgo was able to capitalize on this to exert great influence over the rule of her father, King Cleomenes, and then her husband, King Leonidas I. It is alleged that she deciphered a secret code on a wooden wax tablet that helped stop a planned invasion, making her perhaps one of the world's first female cryptoanalysts!

A relief profile said to be of Gorgo of Sparta.

Hypatia (370–415CE)

Hypatia (370–415CE) was a great mathematician, astronomer and philosopher who lived in the intellectual and cultural hub of Alexandria. Renowned for her public lectures and teachings as head of the Platonist school at Alexandria, she attracted students from across the ancient world and published highly respected commentaries on mathematical principles, along with her own improved techniques. Hypatia lived in a strongly divided city and held significant influence with Alexandria's political and religious elite. Towards the end of her life, she was an advisor to Orestes, the Roman prefect of Alexandria, who was in a political feud with Cyril, the bishop of Alexandria. Rumours spread that she was further dividing Orestes from Cyril.

This coupled with the threat that Hypatia presented as a highly intellectual woman. In March 415, she was murdered by a fanatical Christian mob – an event that marked a turning point for the decline of Alexandria as a centre of great learning.

A painted terracotta figurine of Hypatia.

THE WOMEN OF SPARTA

Unlike Athenian women, who navigated intense male suppression, women in the city-state of Sparta had far more rights and freedoms. They could pursue an education, own and inherit property, control family finances, initiate divorce, play sports, perform music and dance. Most of these opportunities held an ulterior motive: it was believed that physically and intellectually fit women would produce strong male offspring for the battlefield. Spartan women's rights were also enabled by the inequalities of the *helot* system of slavery, whereby those conquered by the Spartans provided all manner of arduous domestic, agricultural and labour support. This in fact has been an unfortunate pattern throughout feminist movements: the dehumanizing system of slavery has often been used by aristocratic women to attain greater freedoms and rights for themselves – on the literal backs of others.

Spartan women were regarded as great athletes who took part in competitive sporting events, including wrestling, running, javelin throwing and horse riding. The Spartan princess Cynisca scooped the first-prize laurels for chariot racing at the Olympic Games in 396BCE, followed by the acclaimed female Spartan equestrian Euryleonis two decades later.

Women in ancient Greece found many ways to navigate extreme patriarchal authority and access an education, one of which was as an educated courtesan or *hetaira*. Athenian women were banned from formal education, but *hetairai* were highly educated and able to leave their domestic confines to debate politics, philosophy, religion and the arts as participants with men in literary symposia. They attended plays, banquets and drinking parties, and often lived independently in their own apartments. Generally, they were foreign-born or freedwomen who were formerly slaves, and quite often of a higher social standing. *Hetairai* were the closest many woman could get to independence in male-dominated ancient Greece, but they often had to sexually pander to men in order to do so. *Hetairai* are frequently referred to as prostitutes, albeit a distinctive type of high-class prostitutes who provided sexual and intellectual companionship for their

male clients. Yet, free *hetairai* could become very wealthy and control their finances, and were the only women permitted seats at male-dominated tables.

Aspasia of Athens (470–410BCE) was a celebrated intellectual and hetaira. From an aristocratic family, she was a teacher of rhetoric and a writer who became the companion of the Athenian statesman Pericles. Her house was an intellectual centre in Athens that attracted some of the most prominent philosophers and writers of the time, including the famed philosopher Socrates. Pericles might have made demeaning claims over women but in reality, Aspasia exerted a great deal of influence as his consort: some called her the unofficial ruler of Athens. Socrates credited her with making Pericles a great orator and improving his own rhetorical skills. Aspasia boldly surpassed the limitations for women by also establishing a renowned school for upper-class Athenian girls.

Rural women and the agrarian question

A great deal of what we know about women at this time – and in ancient civilizations as a whole – centres on accounts of elite women, whereas those of lower status are eclipsed from historical records. The position of agrarian and poorer women is likely to have been quite different. They were probably much freer than the wealthy elite. Without slaves, they would have been more involved in the workforce and carried out an array of agricultural tasks. Many rural women would have been expected to harvest produce and sell it at market. Indeed, written accounts describe low-class women working in retail trade and textile manufacture.

Greek goddesses: empowered or oppressed?

The Greek pantheon is filled with powerful women not subject to the same level of patriarchal control as women in ancient Greece. In fact, in Greek mythology, the very origin of the world is rooted in femininity. Gaia, Mother Earth, emerged when the world was in a state of chaotic nothingness. From her came Uranus (the sky) and the other primordial gods.

In Greek mythology, Pandora, the first woman on Earth, is held responsible for releasing all the evils and vices of humanity into the world: much like the Christian biblical Eve.

Greek mythology comprises numerous deities, but there are 12 main gods who rule Mount Olympus: five are female rulers who hold as much power as their male counterparts. At the same time, they share in many of the oppressions of mortal women, including routine violence, infidelities and glaring injustices. The Greek myths often concentrate on their relationships with men: supporting Greek mortal heroes, being sexually pursued by male gods and mortals, or following male orders.

It is little wonder that Greek mythology reflects – and probably reinforced – a patriarchal system: the majority of Greek myths were transcribed by men, appearing in written form in the works of the Greek male poets Homer and Hesiod. Yet many of the female characters are still immensely inspiring and provide some evidence of the world Greek women navigated, even as their deeds and exploits often went unrecorded.

The goddesses and gods of Mount Olympus live within a patriarchal order established by Zeus.

Marble statue of Athena from the city that bears her name. She bears a shield and carries a spear (unseen).

Athena: goddess of wisdom and war

Athena is the Olympian patroness of the great city of Athens itself. She was born in unusual circumstances. Her father Zeus found out that his next child might overthrow him and therefore swallowed Metis, her mother, while she was already pregnant with Athena. Having done this, Zeus began to experience tremendous headaches. Hephaestus, the god of blacksmiths and fire, struck him with his axe to provide some relief and out leapt Athena from Zeus's head, fully grown and wearing an entire set of armour.

Her road to becoming the patron of ancient Greece's most prosperous city, Athens, is a major instance of a woman triumphing over a man in Greek mythology. Athena's uncle, Poseidon, the god of the sea, claimed that Athens would benefit far more under his stewardship. Poseidon struck a rock with his trident, making a spectacular salty stream well up across the city. Athena, on the other hand, thought carefully and instead planted an olive tree. The first king of Athens, Cecrops, judged that the olive tree was far more beneficial, providing Athenians with fruit, oil and wood, so Athena became the city's patron.

Artemis: goddess of the hunt

One of the most widely venerated Greek deities, particularly in ancient Sparta, Artemis, goddess of the hunt, is the protector of young girls and women. She is the daughter of the Titan goddess Leto and Zeus, the Olympian king of all gods. Legend has it that as soon as she was born, she helped her mother give birth to her twin brother Apollo, which accounts for her role as a goddess of childbirth. For female deities in Greek myths, unlike the male gods, one of the only forms of freedom was celibacy. Artemis, like Athena, was known as a virginal goddess. She inflicted vengeance on men who threatened her chastity: when she found the hunter Actaeon watching her bathing naked, she transformed him into a stag, whereupon he was killed by his hounds. The queen of beasts or 'she of the wild', Artemis is universally depicted as a hunter carrying a bow and arrows, often accompanied by an animal.

Artemis, with a sheaf of arrows and having captured a small stag.

Hera: goddess of women and family

As queen of the gods and another of the 12 Olympians, Hera, goddess of women and family, rules over Mount Olympus together with her husband Zeus. She serves as the protector of married women: her name itself translates as 'protectoress'. Hera is a strong and powerful figure; however, she is all too often represented as jealous and vengeful against the many infidelities of Zeus. Unlike in other mythologies, where such inequalities go unmentioned or are glossed over by highly unrealistic – even if seemingly empowering – representations, Hera, the goddess responsible for family, suffers in an unhappy marriage, must trick her husband to receive sexual attention, and is frequently cheated on by a husband who goes unpunished. In the history of feminism, this can be interpreted as a description of the realities of family life in an extremely patriarchal society. Greek society was structured in such a way that women were often highly dependent on their husbands and frequently unable to change that misogynist dynamic. However, in myths, Hera does have a chance to wreak her vengeance, even if it is usually on Zeus's female lovers or illegitimate children and not on Zeus himself.

Shifting boundaries

After Alexander the Great, during the period of ancient Greece known as Hellenistic Greece, the city-states fell into rapid decline. By all accounts, this led to increased freedoms for Greek women. In response to growing poverty, many began to work outside the home. The orator Demosthenes wrote in the fourth century BCE of women working as nurses, fruit pickers and wool workers as a result of the city's penury.

The ancient Greek empire finally came to an end at the hands of the new superpower of ancient Rome. Nevertheless, Greek civilization had a strong influence on Roman civilization: many historians describe the Roman era as Graeco-Roman because it so firmly continued many of the elements of the ancient Greek era. At the start, rights for women in ancient Rome were relatively similar to those of women in ancient

Hera is shown here bearing a vessel of water and the apple of discord.

Greece. Yet over the 500 years that Rome held sway as an empire, the revolution for women gathered speed and women would achieve greater economic independence and the relaxation of ideological and physical constraints.

Women in ancient Rome

The Roman Empire spanned much of Europe, northern Africa and western Asia. Beginning with the rise of the city of Rome in 753BCE, it lasted well over 1,000 years, until the fifth century CE.

Like the ancient Greek society that preceded it, ancient Rome was also a misogynist society in which women still had few of the rights of male citizens. Roman women could not hold political power directly, nor could they vote. However, the rights and status of women eased significantly over the later years of the Roman Empire. Then, women could own property, write their own wills and put forward legal cases. Those from prominent wealthy families were able to exert powerful influence behind the scenes. Some did so within prescribed gender roles as wives, mothers, lovers, daughters or sisters. Others pushed back on these roles altogether and achieved political, religious and military power.

Domestic greatness

Women in most ancient civilizations played pivotal roles in the everyday life of their households. By focusing on the recorded spectacular achievements of women in political, economic and cultural spheres, it is easy to discount the many women who might not have achieved recorded greatness, but who were no less great in their own ways. As in ancient Greece and Egypt, the majority of women were responsible for leading the everyday affairs of their households and entertaining guests. In aristocratic families, where men were away on military campaigns or administrative duties for long periods, women would often take care of the property and finances, too.

RIGHT: A Roman fresco showing a woman painting a statue of Priapus, found in the Casa del Chirurgo in Pompeii.

ABOVE: A portrait of an elegant Roman woman from the second century CE.

THE VESTAL VIRGINS

One of the few public roles that women alone could hold was in the priestly office of the Vestal Virgins. However, there were only six of them, so the odds were slim on being a Vestal! The Vestals led very different lives to their contemporaries. At a young age, Vestal Virgins were selected from highborn families and granted privileges that were unimaginable for most women in ancient Rome: they could vote, own property and write a will, attend public athletic displays, and free condemned prisoners and slaves. However, this came at a great cost. For 30 years, they were sworn to celibacy and had to devote their lives to the study and observance of rituals said to be essential for Rome's survival, such as tending to the sacred fire of Vesta, the Roman goddess of the hearth, one of the most important deities.

A Roman statue of a Vestal Virgin, dating from the second century CE.

Layers of suppression

The violent system of slavery was integral to establishing the Roman Empire as an economic power. It is important to remember that the power that women exerted in domestic spaces often relied on the subordination of others. Women in ancient Rome could buy, sell, inherit and free slaves and, depending on their status, often managed a household of servants and slaves. Slaves came primarily from Rome's military expansion across Europe and the Mediterranean. As a slave, you were considered property under Roman law, without any legal or indeed real personhood.

A mosaic of a Roman matron in her toilet room with attendant slaves, fourth century CE.

SOCIALIZING AT THE *THERMAE*

The Romans adopted many bathing practices from the Greeks, including developing the bath or *thermae* as a social and recreational hub. Communal bathing at the local spa played a big part in the social calendar of women and men alike in ancient Rome. Women were not often seen away from the home outside of religious occasions so bathhouses were important sites for women across social classes to meet publicly. Far more than places to soak, bathhouses allowed women to spend time together, debate politics and literary texts, make business transactions, plan social events and meet lovers. Public baths spread across the Roman Empire and are still popular to this day in North Africa, the Mediterranean and Europe.

BEAUTY IN ANCIENT ROME

In common with the ancient Egyptians and Greeks, for many Roman women cosmetics played a crucial part in daily rituals and were arguably important tools of expression and self-empowerment. However, fragments from Ovid's *Medicamina Faciei Femineae* (*Women's Facial Cosmetics*) reveal some of the extreme practices that women engaged in to conform to feminine beauty ideals being popularized at the time. This book contains recipes on making your skin whiter and getting rid of pimples. In 2003, archaeologists discovered Roman face cream at a site near London that consisted of a mixture of animal fat, resins and highly toxic lead. Researchers debate the effects this might have had on the aristocracy in particular, who often had their own beauticians; it is thought that lead possibly exacerbated mortality and reduced fertility.

A bust of Livia Drusilla from the National Archaeological Museum in Athens.

Indirect political rule

The most well-known of ancient Rome's influential women were born of aristocratic families and were keen politicians behind the scenes. Their impact illustrates another of the major ways that, along with holding priestly offices, women excluded from direct rule could rule indirectly.

Livia Drusilla (58BCE–29CE)

As the wife of Emperor Augustus and born into a wealthy family, Livia Drusilla (58BCE–29CE) was arguably the most politically influential woman across the Roman Empire. A number of letters between the couple remain from that time, revealing the power that Livia had on Augustus's decision making as he dramatically expanded the empire. Livia held the right to manage her own financial affairs without a guardian and was given the protection of the state or *sacrosancitas*. Livia's political power was resented by many Roman politicians and she is often much maligned. She is rumoured to have been responsible for arranging the deaths of many of Augustus's relatives in order to leverage for her son Tiberius, from her first marriage to Nero, to be adopted as heir. Augustus rarely came under the same tainted brush.

Fulvia (83–40BCE)

Fulvia (83–40BCE) was born into a wealthy republican plebeian family. Fulvia held a notable interest in politics and her public voice became increasingly strong over time. Her political savviness and own birth into the Fulvii political dynasty led to her three successive marriages to politicians close to Julius Caesar. She is most famous for her role in propelling Mark Antony's career and her commanding rule over a number of legions in the Perusine War of 41–40BCE. Fulvia was the first Roman woman to be featured on Roman coins.

Two sides of a coin showing Fulvia found in the city of Eumeneia (later renamed Fulvia) in Phrygia.

A 'NASTY WOMEN' MARCH

At the height of the Second Punic War (218–201 BCE) between the two major western Mediterranean powers of Carthage and Italy, Roman officials introduced a series of laws called *Lex Oppia* in 215BCE to regulate public consumption and extravagance. This included statutes on dinner expenditure, as well as a law that specifically restricted the wealth of women and their display of wealth. For example, no woman could possess more than 12 g (1/2 oz) of gold, wear a multicoloured garment (especially if it was trimmed in purple!) or ride in carriages, except for religious occasions. The women of Rome took to the streets to protest, courageously showing their power in an intensely patriarchal society. Although their demands might seem superficial, personal adornment was one of the few avenues Roman women had to proclaim their identity and hold personal wealth. Women streamed into Rome from rural areas and towns to show their outrage. Concerted activism, demonstrations at and around the Roman Forum, and advocacy with consuls and officials eventually led to *Lex Oppia* being revoked in 195BCE, 20 years after its initial passing. At the time, the women were denounced in the Senate as 'uncontrollable' and 'untamed creatures'. Think how this bears parallels to the 'nasty woman' phrase that became a women's-rights rallying call in response to Donald Trump's remarks against Hillary Clinton.

ROMAN WOMEN IN BUSINESS

Excavations at the volcanic site of Pompeii have provided insights into women's role in business enterprises in the later days of the Republic. Eumachia of Pompeii (first century CE), for instance, owned a successful brick-making business, which did so well that she purchased a number of public buildings across the city, including this majestic building, which likely housed the fullers' cloth-working guild. Eumachia herself was made a public priestess of Venus during the first century CE and exerted a great deal of local political influence through this public office.

The decline of the Roman Empire

The Roman Empire slowly fell after a series of challenges that eventually divided its vast territory into a number of successor polities. By 476CE, the Western Roman Emperor held little military, political or financial control over the dispersed regions of the empire, allowing other kingdoms to establish their own power. In that same year, Germanic King Odoacer finally deposed Romulus Augustulus, the last emperor of the Western Roman Empire in Italy.

The women rulers of the Maya empire

The Maya empire was centred in the region of modern-day south-eastern Mexico, Guatemala, Belize, Honduras and El Salvador. Beginning around 2000BCE, the Maya civilization is known for the monumental architecture of its cities, its sophisticated hieroglyphic writing and calendar systems, agricultural cultivation, mathematics and astronomical expertise. Many of the great Maya cities were abandoned by 900CE, but the descendants of the Maya number more than six million people, who speak over 28 surviving Mayan languages and live in the same region as their ancestors.

While the ancient Egyptian, Greek then Roman empires were jostling among one another, across the Atlantic another great civilization was prospering. Prior to Spanish conquest, the Maya were the dominant society of the western hemisphere. The term 'Maya' is collectively used nowadays to describe the many people that inhabited the region, but the Maya did not have a common political unity. Instead, their society consisted of a number of

The Maya are famous for several warrior queens. This is Ix Ek' Naah or Lady Star House, who was also known as the Snake Lady of Palenque. She was a Maya queen of the Kaan kingdom in Campeche. In this famous altar stone from modern-day Guatemala, she wears the helmet of the Maya god of war and stands atop a large battle platform. The infamous Kaan or Snake dynasty rose to great power and influence across the rainforests of the Yucatán Peninsula.

independent city-states that included rural farming communities and large urban hubs. They were skilled farmers, clearing vast areas of tropical rainforest for the cultivation of corn, beans, squash and cassava. They developed extensive trade networks that connected architecturally innovative city-states. In their cities, Maya employed novel urban planning to arrange pyramids, temples and marketplaces according to a grid system. Across what archaeologists call the Classic period, between 250 and 900CE, the Maya civilization flourished throughout Central America.

Women were central to Mayan society: as rulers and in all aspects of the economy. Each of the Maya city-states was ruled by a hierarchical system of government of nobles and royalty, underneath which operated a strict social caste system. Men tended to be kings and rulers of the city-states, but there were a number of women who gained political power, ruling as queens of their city-states. The first widely known Maya leader was Lady Yohl Ik'nal (d. 604) or Lady Heart of the Wind Place, of the great city-state of Palenque in southern Mexico. Her reign was impressive: she withstood two crippling attacks from the neighbouring Calakmul and Bonampak, but still held on to power. She was venerated throughout her reign, ruling for a full 21 years until her death.

Well-known Mayan female rulers of the Classic period also include the Lady of Tikal, Muwaan Mat of Palenque, Lady Eveningstar of Yaxchilan, and Lady K'abel of the Waka kingdom. Of these queens, Lady Six Sky of Naranjo (682–741CE) – also known as Lady Wak Chanjalam Lem – had a particularly impressive reign. Originally a princess from the powerful Dos Pilas city-state, Lady Six Sky was sent to establish a new dynasty at the lesser kingdom of Naranjo in the Petén region of north-eastern Guatemala. Many of her exploits are depicted in stone monuments and tablets. She launched at least eight major military campaigns, one of which is recorded in a representation of her as a warrior queen standing over a captive. She also commissioned monuments that detail the important calendric rituals she carried out, such as ones aligning with the moon's cycles.

During the Classic era, while some women held power as the rulers of city-states, others served as oracular priestesses. For the ancient Maya, ritualized bloodletting or ch'ahb' was an important way for the nobles to communicate with their royal ancestors and gods. Within the Mesoamerican belief system, bloodletting legitimized the ruling lineage's position in power. Typically performed by elites and religious figures, rituals would be publicly enacted atop pyramids or on elevated platforms, where the local population could congregate. Some early murals, such as those from Bonampak in the southern Mexican state of Chiapas, depict women engaging in bloodletting rituals, including one in which noblewomen hold stingray spines to their tongues.

The queen Lady K'abel of the Waka city-state – known as Lady Snake Lord and Lady Waterlily-Hand – in the northern Guatemalan Petén region is shown in ceremonial headdress in this 2.74-m- (9-ft-) tall limestone monument.

ABOVE: The signature insignia of
Lady Yohl Ik'nal.

RIGHT: In this limestone stela,
Lady Six Sky is dressed in
maize god and moon goddess
regalia, which shows her to be
both a triumphant ruler and
ritual priestess. The name 'Six'
is associated with the maize god.
Here, she stands on a bound
captive from the small polity of
K'inichkaab. She is described
on the side of the stela tablet
as ub'aah ti yax k'uh or 'she
is portrayed as the first god',
meaning that she was regarded
as a vessel for this god.

BELOW: Tikal was the capital of one of the most powerful ancient Maya kingdoms. Situated in the
northern Guatemalan Petén region, the great city-state had a series of dynastic rulers, including
Queen Unen Bahlam (c.317CE) and the famous Lady of Tikal, who ruled from the age of seven
at around 511 to 527CE. The monumental architecture of Tikal's urban centre dates back to the
fourth century BCE. During the Classic period, the city dominated the Maya region. It is now a
UNESCO World Heritage Site and is one of the largest archaeological sites of Maya civilization.

In this Maya limestone carving from Yaxchilan in Chiapas, known as lintel 24 (c.723CE), the Maya Queen Lady Xoc is depicted performing a ritual sacrifice in which she draws a barbed rope through her tongue.

Ixchel was the primary Maya moon goddess. A fearsome goddess, married to the sun god, she was also the patron of medicine, fertility and childbirth. Mayan mythology often associated the moon with a woman accompanied by a rabbit: a symbol of fertility, abundance and new beginnings. In Isla Mujeres in the Mexican Yucatán, there is a temple dedicated to Ixchel. Local legend states that when Spanish colonists arrived at the island they saw the representation of Ixchel and many offerings of female statues to the goddess, and called the island Isla Mujeres or 'Island of Women'. Ixchel inhabits the land of mists and rainbows and so is often also referred to as 'rainbow woman'.

The ancient Maya were keen astronomers and made meticulous records and interpretations of planetary movements from large observatories. Many of their administrative and ceremonial complexes were laid out with astronomical observations in mind. Mayan understandings of the sun, moon and planets, including that of Venus and Mars, inspired their famous calendar. Agricultural activities were timed to coincide with particular astronomical arrangements and Mayan women held positions of political power based on these cosmologies, which gave crucial roles to female and male divinities.

Women were economic powerhouses in the Mayan economy, especially in agriculture and the textile industry. Farming was the principle focus for the majority of people, elites and commoners alike. Anthropologists believe that farm work was not designated as solely male or female among the Maya. Often fields were farmed collaboratively. As farmers, women produced widely traded food products such as cacao and vanilla beans. They engaged in farm work such as the planting, weeding and harvesting of corn. In some Mayan regions, women were herders and raised deer to feed the population. In cases where hunting, food production and processing might be divided between women and men, these tasks were likely to be taken together as integral parts of the overall production process, and not represented along a gender divide.

The Bonampak murals (c.790CE) vividly capture the reign of the city's last ruling family, King Chan Muwan and Lady Rabbit. Scenes depict women and men using stringray and cactus spines and obsidian knives to engage in bloodletting rituals. These murals also give important evidence of gender ambiguity in Maya society. Maya probably had a very different perception of gender to a contemporary Western male–female binary. Many images of Maya rulers have fluid mixed-gender characteristics, such as the amalgamation of the maize god and moon goddess into one revered deity. Even the maize deity is often depicted with a male upper body and female lower body or as gender ambiguous.

THE ANCIENT ART OF MAYAN TEXTILES

Mayan women are renowned for their textile arts, and some of the earliest textiles date back to around 1000BCE. Weaving has historically been central to the economic prosperity of Mayan women and their families. As weavers, spinners and dyers, women produced elaborate woven textiles for local markets and trade networks. Textiles also held spiritual significance and were used for ritual purposes.

Most Mayan clothing was made on small looms that were light and portable, tied between the weaver's body and a stationary post (backstrap looms): a technique that is still in use to this day. The bright colours of Mayan cloth were extracted from the natural world, including purple dye from marine molluscs, blue dye from indigo plants and red dye from the small cochineal insects that live on cacti. The woven shapes and distinctive designs often corresponded to particular regions. Motifs can even tell stories of a town's history that goes back generations.

A Mayan woman weaving traditional textiles on a simple loom.

Rigoberta Menchú Tum (b. 1959) is Quiché Maya and one of the most well-known indigenous rights activists in the world. Menchú lived through the horrors of Guatemala's genocidal civil war against the Maya. Her father, mother and brother were all tortured and then murdered by the military. She has focused her life's work on publicizing indigenous rights internationally and was the first indigenous women to receive the Nobel Peace Prize, in 1992. She co-founded the Nobel Women's Initiative, which concentrates on combatting violence against women.

During the Spanish conquest of Guatemala (1524–1821), the Maya experienced extreme persecution. Guatemala's 36-year civil war (1960–96) was partially the result of the US government's attempt to gain control over banana plantations from indigenous ownership. Hundreds of thousands of Indigenous Maya were killed or disappeared, and many more were forced into exile under explicitly genocidal policies. Mayan women bore the brunt of these racist strategies. Maya survivors are still lobbying for justice, and the prosecution of wartime sexual violence against Mayan women is only now underway.

THE LADY OF CAO AND THE TRANSGENDER FLUIDITY OF THE MOCHE

The Moche civilization flourished from 100 to 700 CE along the western coast of northern Peru. In 2006, Peruvian archaeologists discovered a 1,500-year-old female Moche mummy, known as the Lady of Cao. She was buried with her wealth and jewellery along with two priests, two bodyguards and a teenage girl in a splendid 280-sq-m (3,000-sq-ft) tomb at the sacred Cao Viejo temple complex.

Archaeologists now surmise that the Lady of Cao held the most prominent position in Moche civilization in the fourth and fifth centuries. As a ruler and high priestess, she would have dominated administrative, political and religious affairs across the Chicama River valley. Owing to the salty sea air of the tomb's location, her body is incredibly well preserved. Magnificent tattoos adorn her forearms and hands, including figures of serpents that signify her religious power as an oracle and great healer, as well as spiders, showcasing her talent as a weaver. Her tomb is filled with finely worked gold, copper and silver, and decorated with murals of divine creatures from the Moche cosmology.

The Lady of Cao was not the only evidence of the prominent role of women in Moche society. Since the discovery, a number of royal tombs have been found containing elite priestesses wearing exquisite headdresses and beaded necklaces, and surrounded by valuable treasures such as silver goblets, as well as sacrificial victims. Their elaborate burials indicate the high status of the women, who were among the most important people in their society.

The discovery of the Lady of Cao and other powerful priestess rulers refutes previous beliefs that Moche civilization was patriarchal or male dominated. Many of these previous assumptions were levelled by male archaeologists, who transplanted their Western gender ideologies on to very different cultures. In her essay 'Towards a Transgender Archaeology', the anthropologist Mary Weismantel argues that archaeologists should move away from projecting Western dichotomies on to complex past societies that

A *model of the Lady of Cao: her face was reconstructed using* 3D *scanning and printing techniques.*

Thousands of Moche 'sex pots' have been discovered, which provide evidence of different conceptions towards gender and sexuality.

might have experienced the world in very different ways: perhaps ones in which the dichotomy between men in power and women being dominated makes little sense.

That the Moche had very different conceptions of gender and sexuality is also evident in their celebrated pottery or 'sex pots'. These erotic ceramic vessels, uncovered in spiritual temples and royal tombs across Peru's northern coast, show a wide range of sexual acts. Intimacy is depicted between sexes, and it is often difficult to distinguish the sex or gender of individuals.

The ancient civilizations of Mesoamerica, Egypt, Greece and Rome had a sweeping influence on the world that we are familiar with today. These are still exhibited across the fields of language, art, literature, infrastructure, government practices and legal systems. Women were often given little credit or their role has been limited to gender stereotypes of passivity and domesticity, and all too often devalued. However, women young and old played a tremendous part of these ancient civilizations, succeeding, despite immense limitations in some overtly patriarchal cultures, in becoming agents of social change. This was not only the case in the Mediterranean and Mesoamerica but, as later chapters will show, extended to great civilizations around the world.

Strict divisions in ancient and imperial China existed between men and women. Although holding limited political rights and being restricted to domestic spaces across many Chinese regions, women developed exclusive female-centred occupations and cultivated academic and literary circles, especially during the Ming dynasty (1368–1644).

Chapter
2 MATRIARCHIES AND THE MIDDLE AGES

The Middle Ages or medieval era commonly refers to the period in Europe between the fall of the Roman Empire in 476CE and the dawn of the 14th-century Renaissance. With Europe no longer governed under a single empire, dramatic changes occurred in the region's structure and social climate, including mass migration, shifts in languages away from Latin, and the spread of Christianity and Islam. However, these changes were not just specific to Europe. This period was also one of great developments and flourishing cultures across Asia, Africa, the Americas and Oceania. Many of these regions were also physically and intellectually connected through cosmopolitan trading networks.

Evil temptresses and virginal goddesses: the Middle Ages and the Church

Women played an important part in the significant advances that occurred at this time. In much of Europe, women battled extreme discrimination thanks to gender norms solidified by the Church. However, a number of key figures challenged the patriarchal system and leveraged more openings towards advancing egalitarian participation. In addition, more women started to record their experiences and express their opinions in writing. This represented a great advancement from when most early accounts of women were written by men. Furthermore, in other global contexts during the medieval era, women wielded greater authority over men. Among some West African ethnolinguistic groups, for example, female political rulers were just as common as male leaders. Looking at the medieval time period, with all its shifts in society and political structures, reveals quite how far we have come and the women who helped make this possible.

Women's lives in Europe during the Middle Ages were heavily governed by the Church and the aristocratic system. The Church gave people an understanding of the meaning of life and their place in it. Meanwhile, the aristocracy governed people's place within a rigid social hierarchy known as the feudal system. Society was stratified into the classes of clergy, nobility and serfs (or peasantry), all of whom were tied together through the manorial system. In this arrangement, the lord of the manor ruled a large estate worked on by the serfs, who were kept secure in exchange for their toil. The position of women within this feudal system was one of subservience. The lord controlled whom the peasantry bound to their land could marry. Once married, a woman's husband often controlled her

The Middle Ages is usually divided into three periods:

1. Early Middle Ages – 476–1000
2. High Middle Ages – 1000–1300
3. Late Middle Ages – 1300–1500

interests. However, despite societal restrictions, some women in the Middle Ages led nuanced and varied lives that were very different to the stereotypes of damsels in distress or dutiful women in the fields.

During the Middle Ages, women's place in society was ostensibly decreed by biblical texts. As Christianity spread rapidly across Europe during the fourth century, the Bible was given greater authority and women's status soon fell. According to biblical accounts, Eve was created from the rib of Adam and was guilty of causing man's expulsion from paradise by eating the forbidden fruit. A great deal of medieval art depicts women as responsible for 'original sin', even to the extent of depicting the serpent who tempts Eve with a female head! This story has long been marshalled to reinforce a belief in women's inferiority, as an allegedly morally weaker, deceitful temptresses who would sway men into committing abominable sins.

On the other side of the character trope of women as sinful Eve lies the Virgin Mary: the mother of Jesus Christ. During the Middle Ages, the Virgin Mary was taken to be the ultimate female archetype and a model of motherhood and chastity. In Christianity, Mary pledged to virginity and conceived her child Jesus miraculously through the power of the Holy Spirit without sexual relations. According to this character ideology, the primary duty of women was to remain virtuous – connecting to the popularized role of women in medieval European society as mother and childbearer.

Counter to idealized representations as virgin/mother or reviled depictions as temptress, women from all social classes were involved in a variety of active roles in medieval Europe.

Art and literature created throughout the Middle Ages represented women either as the embodiment of sin or as models of chastity and motherhood.

THE MADONNA-WHORE COMPLEX

Many early male explanations for human behaviour are highly problematic, but also revealing of thought at the time. The madonna-whore complex is an interesting theory put forward by the psychologist Sigmund Freud in the early 20th century that demonstrates the power early Virgin-Eve representations can hold in the present. According to this theory, men see women as either pure, nurturing and asexual (the Virgin) or as tainted, promiscuous and sexual (Eve): loving the first but desiring the second. These dichotomous representations encourage women to be either 'virginal' or sexual, but never both. Freud used this concept to explain the difficulty of men and women in maintaining sexual arousal within loving relationships. Freud's argument is equally problematic because it places the 'blame' squarely on women and female sexuality. He also linked the roots of this dichotomy to men's unresolved sensual feelings towards their mothers. However, feminist critics argue that it is instead connected to cultural and social belief systems designed to reinforce unequal gender roles. Such polarized perceptions of women also speak to the continued demonization of women's freedom of sexual expression. Women still experience double standards for the same sexual behaviour displayed by many men.

In Olivuccio di Ciccarello's painting The Madonna of Humility with the Temptation of Eve (c.1400), *the pure Virgin Mary sits holding the infant Jesus, while the naked Eve lies below with a serpent wrapped around her thigh as the counter representation of lust and temptation.*

Eve, the creator of original sin, thus provided the argument for why women should be obedient and suppressed, while the Virgin Mary provided the model to aspire to: a dutiful wife and mother. Neither of these dichotomous interpretations allowed for an understanding of women as individuals.

Although women were recording their experiences in greater numbers, histories remain skewed towards male accounts and voices in the medieval period in Europe. However, we know that women in the era certainly did not passively accept religious and political misogyny. Many women participated in crucial industries, often working alongside their husbands as tenant farmers in the fields in addition to performing domestic work.

Medieval guilds

Guilds were influential community associations organized around trades or crafts across Europe in the Middle Ages. Functioning like a modern-day trade union, guilds controlled that industry's operation in the region. Most medieval guilds limited women's participation, despite the fact that many were highly skilled artisans. However, groups of driven women in France and Germany developed exclusively female and incredibly powerful silk and textile guilds. These provided a platform for them to protect their economic interests, along with offering political clout and social privilege.

Isaac van Swanenburg painted workers of the wool trade in Leiden, the Netherlands, in 1595.

Saint Hildegard of Bingen (1098–1179) was a 12th-century German Benedictine abbess and feminist icon. She founded all-female monasteries at Rupertsberg and Eibingen to wrest power away from male religious authority and enable the many nuns alongside her to advance vibrant intellectual lives. Saint Hildegard was a true polymath who excelled across fields of study. She wrote works on theology, botany, zoology and medicine, as well as poetry. She is one of the best-known composers of medieval monophonic music, leaving behind more medieval chants than any other composer in the entire Middle Ages, many of which are popular to this day.

Shattering stained-glass ceilings

Despite the overwhelming restrictions, there were a number of ways in which women in medieval society exercised substantial influence. Ironically, in the Church, women held powerful positions. Some used these spaces to gain religious prestige for women and even, in the case of Hildegard of Bingen (right), achieve sainthood. Female sanctity allowed women to exercise huge authority, including founding nunneries as spaces for female education. As abbesses of convents, women had seniority over communities of both men and women. What's more, far from functioning just as places of worship, religious houses were often centres of scientific ingenuity. Writing was one of these new technologies and it allowed people to collect and share knowledge. At the heart of this groundbreaking work were women, many of whom were highly educated scribes and involved in all manner of manuscript production and technological experimentation. Female literacy subsequently spread from convents to royalty and nobility and, eventually, middle and even lower classes.

The stereotypical image of the Crusades is one of a hypermasculine environment, but in reality women took on major roles in Crusader states.

Women, violence and the Crusades

The Crusades were a series of medieval religious wars that occurred from the late 11th to 13th centuries. Organized by European Western Christians, and supported by the Latin Church, their objective was to combat the spread of Islam in the eastern Mediterranean, including the important regions of Syria, Palestine, Egypt and Anatolia. Participation in warfare was largely confined to men, but some women took part in combat, made military decisions and conducted diplomatic negotiations on both Christian and Muslim sides. During the Seventh Crusader attack on Egypt, for example, Shajarat al-Durr (d. 1259), wife of the Egyptian sultan, organized the kingdom's defence. Upon her husband's death, she became the first female sultan, going on to defeat Louis IX of France at Damietta. Meanwhile, on the home front, many women took on substantial roles that were previously unavailable to them, including ruling estates and overseeing agricultural and economic activities.

Beguines were groups of women in north-western Europe, quite radical for their time, who formed unique communities from 1200. Many men left to fight in the Crusade wars, leaving women more administrative power in running socio-economic life. These freedoms, coupled with interests in humanitarian spirituality, inspired groups of women to step out of traditional gender roles and form intentional communities after the Crusades ended. Although they lived together and dedicated themselves to prayer and local philanthropy, Beguines were outside Church regulations. Beguine communities varied from shared houses to entire towns or *beguinages*, some of which are now recognized as UNESCO World Heritage sites. Beguines played a significant role in advancing literacy and the textile industry. They are important examples of all-women communities who sought independence through sisterhood solidarity.

Eleanor of Aquitaine

Queen of France and then England, active participant in a Crusade and patron of the arts, Eleanor of Aquitaine (1122–1204) stands out as a politically savvy power player in medieval Europe. During her first marriage, to Louis VII of France, she took part in the Crusades when few women could, and recruited other women to join her. She left her first marriage and went on to marry King Henry II of England by her own choice, during which time she played a major role in government. She eventually supported her sons in an unsuccessful revolt against their father and was subjected to 16 years of house arrest. When her son Richard I or 'the Lionheart' succeeded to the throne, she was granted powers over English political affairs. She wielded considerable influence as the queen mother and ruler of the kingdom when King Richard went to fight in the Third Crusade.

The 19th-century Pre-Raphaelite artist Frederick Sandys depicted Eleanor of Aquitaine in his movement's typically romantic style.

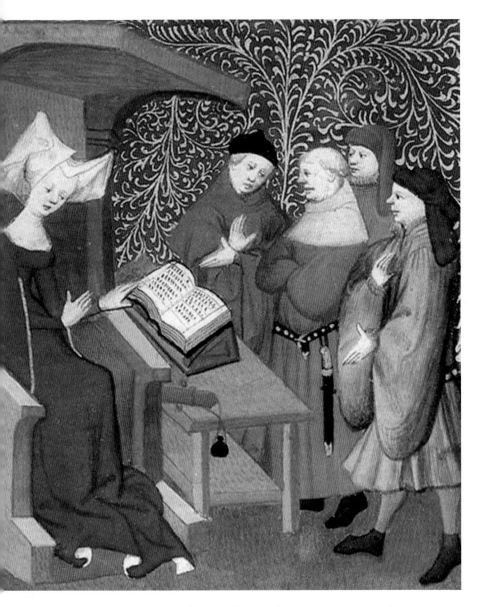

The medieval feminist writer Christine de Pizan lecturing to a group of men.

Christine de Pizan

A prolific French-Italian female writer, Christine de Pizan (1364–c.1430) openly discussed feminist issues in her works, such as women's oppression, access to education and visions of egalitarian society. One of her most celebrated works is *The Book of the City of Ladies* (1405), which chronicles the greatness and accomplishments of women in a symbolic city of women.

The trobairitz were female troubadours in Occitania (a historical region of southern France, Catalonia and Italy) during the 12th and 13th centuries. Trobairitz composed *fin' amors* or songs of courtly love, which would be performed for the nobility, including Eleanor of Aquitaine, who was a major patron. Many of their songs offer an unusual feminist take on love, flipping the male troubadour narrative to make women the romantic pursuers or questioning what makes an ideal partner. Trobairitz are important figures in musical history since they were the first widely known female composers of Western secular music.

Women in ancient and imperial China

A popular saying in imperial China was *nángēngnǚzhì* or 'men plough, women weave'. This idiom described and reinforced historical gender roles in Chinese society, whereby women were expected to stick to domestic realms. However, archaeological evidence from the Neolithic period (8500–2070BCE) suggests that this kind of gendered division of labour did not occur until the rise of pastoralism. Archaeological excavations from the Yangshao culture, which flourished along the Yellow River, revealed agricultural practices were performed mostly by women. Burial rites were egalitarian and sometimes favoured women substantially. This has led to much-debated theories on Yangshao society as matrilineal.

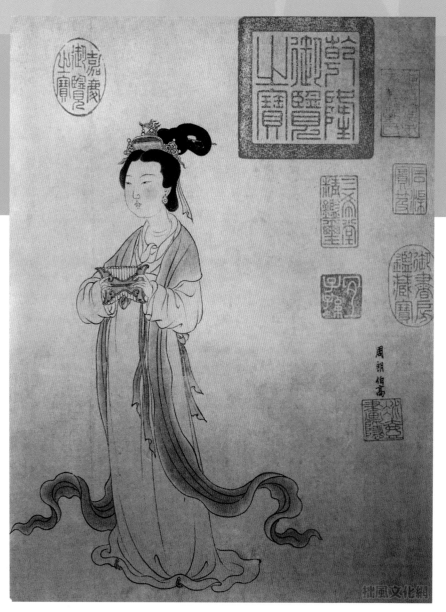

CHINESE DYNASTIES

Chinese history is divided between ancient (8500–256BCE), imperial (221BCE–1912CE) and modern eras (1912–present), within which ruled a succession of hereditary monarchical regimes or 'dynasties'. The Xia dynasty (2070–1600BCE), under Yu the Great, is considered the start of Chinese dynastic rule. In this system, sovereign rulers possessed absolute power of the realm. The throne was technically passed down the male line. However, there were many cases in which women took on de facto power.

As in medieval Europe, women in imperial China were heavily restricted from participating in many public realms of social life. As early as the Zhou dynasty (1046–256BCE), texts such as the *Rites of Zhou* (a work on bureaucratic organization) contained moral principles and social codes of behaviour for female education. This etiquette guide, which formed a core part of female education at the time, included obedience to men and modesty in actions and speech. However, this is not to say that the Zhou ritual guides were stringently followed! Records from this period show women advising men on political strategy. For instance, the first king of the Zhou dynasty, Wu, appointed his wife Yi Jiang as one of his elite political advisors. There are also accounts of a woman advising a man how to shoot correctly. This woman's name was only recorded as 'the wife of the bow artisan' of the state of Jin, illustrating the non-individuality women experienced as male property at this time, but nevertheless, she showed her skills in defiance of male patriarchal norms. This included confronting Duke Ping of Jin, who was all set to execute her husband, the court's bow-and-arrow maker, for the poor quality of his craftsmanship. She used her ingenuity and skills to show that it was not because of the poor quality of the bow that the duke's arrows had failed to land on the target but rather his poor technique. She went on to teach the duke how to properly hold the bow and release the arrow. In exchange, she was rewarded with a sizable sum, while also saving her husband from execution.

Neolithic pottery jar from the Majiayao culture decorated with a figure that has both male and female genitalia, leading archaeologists to conclude that the genders were considered powerful as a whole.

CONFUCIANISM AND GENDER

Confucianism is an ancient system of spiritual thought and life guidance that was developed by the male Chinese philosopher Confucius (551–479BCE). Although not an organized religion, Confucianism became the official Chinese imperial philosophy that was held by almost every feudal dynasty until 1911. Confucian teachings, many of which were collected in *The Analects*, had a dramatic influence on the segregation of women and men. According to Confucian doctrine, 'husband guides wife' (夫为妻纲) and is the decision-maker of the family, much like the king of a state. If these roles were properly followed, Confucius claimed, societal order would be maintained.

Confucianism was declared counter-revolutionary by Chairman Mao when the Communists came to power in 1949, but the philosophy has since seen a huge revival across China and East Asia – and is now endorsed by the Communist Party. There is presently a drive to reinterpret Confucian teachings through the lens of gender equality and humanism.

Yin and yang

The system of yin and yang was developed to explain the universe, as the dark and light principles that exist together harmoniously in human nature. It is pictorially represented by the symbol of Tai Chi. As such, the *yin-yang* (陰-陽) relation is originally a cosmic idea that does not describe human relations such as gender. However, in Confucianized Chinese society, many Confucian scholars took it to signify a natural hierarchical ordering of stereotyped gender relations. Confucian teachings about the subordinate role of women were thus reinforced by their association with *yin* negative qualities of darkness and passivity. According to this line of thought, if *yin* gained the upper hand, cosmic and social order would be endangered. Conceptualizing differences between men and women in this way emphasizes that this is the natural order of the universe, not the social roles artificially created by humans.

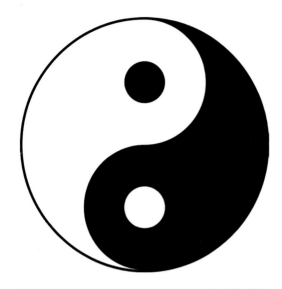

RIGHT: Im YunjiDan (1721–93) was a prominent Korean Confucian scholar. She fought for women's rights as part of her advocacy for a Neo-Confucianism, maintaining that no innate differences exist between men and women. She lobbied for women to have universal access to education and become Confucian masters. Today, the revival of Confucianism in China and East Asia has seen women playing increasingly central roles.

RIGHT: Dr Yu Dan is a media studies professor in Beijing whose Chinese bestselling book Confucius from the Heart: Ancient Wisdom for Today's World (2007) *gives an updated interpretation of Confucian doctrines relevant to contemporary concerns. That a woman is at the centre of the Confucian revival in China speaks volumes to gender advancements in the country, where religious philosophy can in fact be compatible with egalitarian attitudes towards gender.*

Women rulers in the golden age of the Tang Dynasty (618–906CE)

The Tang dynasty is considered the golden age of Chinese culture and economic expansion. Tang China acquired a global reputation as one of the greatest empires in the medieval world, attracting merchants and envoys from across Asia and the Middle East along the Silk Road. Women still navigated a patriarchal system, but this was a time of liberal ideas and relative freedom. In the Tang dynasty, women held high government positions, as well as being able to play polo and other sports with men, drink wine in taverns and carry out business independently.

This was also a period marked by powerful female rulers, including China's only female emperor or *huangdi*, Wu Zetian (r. 690–705CE). During her 40-year reign, she brought the Tang dynasty to the height of its influence. She instituted agricultural reforms and advanced political changes that allowed talented individuals from the lower classes to access government positions. She also reopened the Silk Road trading route and played a pivotal role in the early development of printing. Much controversy surrounds the reign of Wu as a cruel ruler who took ruthless actions against her rivals. There is probably truth in her Machiavellian statecraft, but many hyperbolic narratives could derive from prejudices of male Confucian officials against strong women in power. Although many male emperors glorified themselves like Wu (she called her reign *Tianzhou* or 'granted by heaven') and carried out similarly horrific deeds to stay in power, they are not painted with the same maligned brush. Several other women played crucial roles in state affairs after Wu, including Empress Wei and Princess Taiping.

ABOVE: *Princess Pingyang (590–623CE) kicked off the era of female power. She was the daughter of the first emperor of the Tang dynasty, Emperor Gaozu. She organized and commanded an 'Army of the Lady' to help him seize power from the previous Sui dynasty.*

RIGHT: Wu Zetian (624–705CE) *was the only female emperor in China's imperial history. Her commanding reign was central in China's growth, as she carried out military campaigns to expand its borders. She also instituted agricultural reforms, including lowering taxes on peasants and promoting research to increase agricultural production. Indeed, agricultural production under her reign reached an all-time high.*

CULTURE UNDER THE TANG

Painting, fashion and cosmopolitan culture flourished in the Tang Dynasty. This was a high point for women's fashion with exquisite silk materials and innovative styles developed from trade and cultural exchanges with Korea, Japan, Vietnam and Persia. Low-cut dresses, short sleeves and see-through materials were all popular at the time.

Polo was hugely popular in the Tang dynasty. Terracotta figures of female polo players have been unearthed in China, as well as depictions in paintings and frescoes in excavated tombs. There were also cases of women being buried with their horses! As Confucian teachings grew in popularity with the fall of the Tang dynasty, however, many women had fewer opportunities to take part in public sporting pursuits like polo.

Women in the Incan Empire

The Incan empire or *Tawantinsuyo* ('Land of the Four Quarters') was the largest empire in pre-Columbian America. It arose in the Peruvian highlands in the 12th century and lasted until the Spanish conquest in the 1500s. At its peak, the Incan empire encompassed Peru along with parts of Ecuador, Bolivia, Argentina, Chile and Colombia.

The vast Incan empire was governed from the capital of Cusco in Peru. Andean society was immensely hierarchical and operated through a regimented system of governance. The Incan state was gendered, but through a dual system of authority based largely on class and birth. Within the tiered social structure, women occupied a complementary role to men. At the top of the hierarchy was the Incan king, the Sapa Inca or 'son of the sun', and the Incan queen, the Quoya or 'queen of all women'. The Quoya held immense political power, including the ability to inherit land and animal herds, and oversaw the administration of religious orders.

Descendants of the Inca still speak different dialects of Quechua, a language that originated prior to the Inca but became their lingua franca.

Beneath the dynastic royalty, local nobles or *kurakas* governed small municipalities (*ayllu*) across the empire. *Kurakas* could be women or men. They participated in community decision making and collected tributes (textiles, grain, wares and labour) from their *ayllu* village-like clan, which were used to appease the gods or passed on to the royalty. Outside of the nobility, women could exert economic autonomy, including engaging in trade and inheriting property.

The Incans were unique among other civilizations in that they became one of the greatest regional powers without a typical system of writing, money or public markets, or the use of iron, steel or the wheel. Instead, monumental architecture and an extensive paved road network with aqueducts and suspension bridges were built using stonework, woven grass and other materials. Complex knotted strings or *quipu* were used for record keeping and communication.

ABOVE: *Mama Ocllo was a central figure in Incan mythology. In some legends, she was a daughter of the sun god Inti and moon goddess Mama Killa; in others, the daughter of Viracocha the creator god. She was believed to have founded the Incan capital Cusco together with her husband Manco Cápac. All Incan rulers were said to be their descendants.*

LEFT: *Incan masonry is legendary. It features great slabs of stone closely fitted with beautiful precision without mortar. The famous royal estate of Machu Picchu is a breathtaking example of Incan architecture.*

Knot talk

One of the challenges for archaeologists in learning more about the Inca is that they developed a complex system of knot writing or *quipu* that is still being decoded to this day. As a result, most of what we know is from Spanish colonists, who projected their own patriarchal ways of viewing the world on to a very different social context. *Quipu* consist of cotton or fibre strings of different colours. Depending on the position of the knots, *quipus* recorded details on the population, tax information, calendar details, military strategies, folk stories and poetry. They were a very effective and highly portable method of universal communication between groups spread across great distances and speaking more than 30 different languages. Some *quipus* contain thousands of cords. Many of the knots were destroyed after the Spanish conquest: both by Spanish colonists trying to stamp out Incan culture and by Incans who wanted to hide important information.

A *modern incarnation of the* quipu.

THE *ACLLA* VIRGINS OF THE SUN

Below the nobility were the *acllas* or 'chosen women'. Much like the Vestal Virgins of ancient Greece, *acllas* were a crucial part of Incan religious and political institutions and very privileged in society. *Acllas* were selected at a young age for their intellect, beauty and talent, and cloistered in *acllahuasi* temple convents, known as the 'House of the Chosen Ones'. Prestigious *acllas* were chosen to be chaste priestesses of the sun cult or *mamaconas*. They were highly culturally educated and experts in weaving fine cloth, singing and performing music, brewing ritual *chicha* maize beer offered to the gods in cups of lavish gold, silver and gemstones, and preparing food consumed at important religious festivals. These were all extraordinarily significant acts that endowed the *acllas* with elevated power. Because of their sacred goddess-like position, some *acllas* were gifted as concubines for royalty and warriors. Although less common, some were deified as the ultimate sacrifice for the gods. These acts had less to do with gender subjugation and more to do with the Incan empire, which operated through a system of physical labour and the sacrifice of women and men alike.

Incan textile gold

As with the Maya, textiles had a major economic and political role in Incan society. Cloth was linked to social hierarchy and symbolized wealth and status. Both men and women created textiles, but women (of all social classes) more commonly engaged in this crucial task. Fine cloth was used as a currency and was considered more valuable than gold or silver. When the Inca conquered new territories, exquisite textiles would be presented to the leaders to solidify their acceptance of the Inca as the new rulers. Through the patterns of their highly decorative textiles, women also chronicled important histories.

Venerating the *Mamazara* corn mother

The Inca were agricultural masters. They developed sophisticated irrigation and terracing systems for farming. Canals snaked down and around crop terraces that were cut into the hillsides of the Andes mountains. Together, Incan men and women engaged in complementary labour for agricultural production. The Inca developed hundreds of varieties of resilient crops such as corn, quinoa and potatoes that fed the vast empire.

Corn was the prestige crop of the Inca. According to tradition, it was introduced to the Andean Cusco valley by the Incan queen Mama Ocllo. Women were responsible for upholding her cult. The initiation of the agricultural cycle involved special harvest festivities led by women that venerated the 'corn mother'. Chronicles also suggest that women were responsible for selecting and refining strains of seeds that would provide abundant crops. To this day, many women in Andean communities are still involved in all aspects of the crop cycle, from selecting seeds to planting, harvest, storage and processing.

ABOVE: Andean women farmers continue to use their traditional knowledge and skills to nurture the biodiversity of the Andes, including conserving seeds of local crop varieties.

BELOW: The Incan agricultural system involved vast acreages of crops at high altitude and more temperate climate zones. It also comprised numerous herds of animals, including llamas and alpacas. Women and men tended to these livestock, which were seen as vital to Andean life. They provided wool, meat, leather, transportation and wealth, and they were often ritually sacrificed in religious ceremonies.

MAMA KILLA

In Incan mythology, Mama Killa (in Quechua, *mama* 'mother', *killa* 'moon') was the goddess of the moon. She was the wife of the sun god Inti and mother of Mama Ocllo, the mythical founder of the Incan empire. Many rituals were based on the lunar calendar, making Mama Killa essential for calculating the passage of time. As the goddess of marriage and menstruation, Mama Killa was considered a fierce defender of women. Dedicated temples to her covered in silver were overseen by *mamacona* priestesses and the Quoya, including a great temple in Cusco.

This lady made stones and boulders speak – huacas [sacred stones or places], idols…. She governed more than her husband Manco Capac; the whole city of Cuzco obeyed and respected her throughout her life because with the power of devils [sic] she worked miracles never seen by man…. She was very beautiful, knowledgeable and did much good for the poor people of the city of Cuzco and the kingdom. For this reason the government of her husband grew rather well.

– Felipe Guamán Poma de Ayala (*c*.1535–*c*.1616), a Quechua nobleman who chronicled the maltreatment of the Inca after Spanish colonial conquest

Mama Huaco: the Incan warrior princess

Mama Huaco was the sister of Mama Ocllo and another legendary founder of the Inca Empire. In some legends, she is an alter ego to Mama Ocllo, and the two are joined as one, Mama Ocllohuaco. Mama Huaco is said to have been a fierce warrior and represented female warrior chieftains who led armies into battle. In one story, she catapulted stones at an enemy tribe. After killing one of the tribe members, she cut open his chest and inflated his lungs with her strong breath. As well as wreaking terror on her enemies, she was also a goddess of agricultural production who sowed the first corn and taught women the art of weaving.

BELOW RIGHT: *The Inti Raymi is a traditional religious festival of the Inca Empire to honour the sun god Inti. It celebrates the winter solstice – the shortest day of the year – and the Inca New Year when the hours of daylight lengthen again. In the southern hemisphere, this is celebrated on June 24. The ceremony lasted for nine days and was filled with parades and dances, as well as animal sacrifices to Pachamama to ensure good future harvests. When the Spanish colonists arrived, they banned the ceremony and many other Incan practices, including wearing traditional clothing. Since 1944, an annual theatrical reconstruction of the Inti Raymi has taken place at Saksaywaman near to the original site of celebration in Cusco.*

BELOW LEFT: *Mama Huaco, a fearsome warrior.*

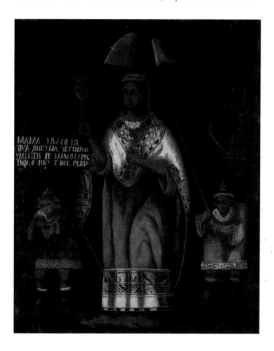

The fall of the Incas

Despite its size and prosperity, the great Inca empire fell to the Spanish conquistadors in the 1500s after just a few centuries of rule. In 1532, when the Spanish conquistador Francisco Pizarro arrived, the Inca empire was wracked by a civil war that had divided the population. Pizarro manipulated the civil unrest to turn some factions against each other. He also learned that the Inca deified their royalty as living gods. Using this understanding, Pizzaro tricked then captured the Incan king Atahualpa (1502–33), forced him to convert to Christianity, and eventually publicly executed him and his family to secure legitimacy for Spanish colonial rule. These forms of ideological domination combined with superior weaponry and the spreading of new diseases, to which the Incans – and other great civilizations of Mesoamerica – had no immunity.

Even after the Spanish conquest, some Inca established small resistance strongholds, including that of Túpac Amaru (1545–72), who was eventually executed after a months-long pursuit. In 1780, two centuries later, Micaela Bastidas Puyucahua (1744–81), a pioneering indigenous leader, led an indigenous independence rebellion against the Spanish in Peru with her husband, José Gabriel Condorcanqui (1738–81) or Túpac Amaru II. She was known as a superior strategist to Túpac Amaru II and was the lead strategist and second-in-command of the rebellion.

A number of women leaders took part in the movement, including Bartolina Sisa (1750–82), who led numerous revolts against the Spanish in present-day Bolivia; José Gabriel's cousin Cecilia Túpac Amaru (1742–83); and Tomasa Tito Condemayta (1729–81), the most powerful chieftain or *cacica* in her region of Acos in Peru. These women leaders re-established the importance of indigenous women in social life and politics, which the Spanish colonists had undermined. Despite numerous successful defences against the armoured Spaniards, all of the rebels were eventually captured and brutally executed. Many are upheld as revolutionary icons of indigenous resistance to this day.

Micaela Bastidas Puyucahua, a revolutionary martyr of Peru.

Matriarchal societies

Matriarchal societies are ones in which women hold overall authority, including key positions in political leadership and socio-economic control. There are some societies that are matrilineal, meaning that a person's lineage is traced through their maternal ancestry. This generally affects how property and assets are passed down through generations or whose surnames and titles are taken. The tracing of kinship through the female line does not necessarily mean that the society is matriarchal. There are, however, a number of matriarchal societies around the world in which women have long been the ones with social privilege.

Challenging Western patriarchal norms

The singer-songwriter Taylor Swift made a powerful statement on the disparities between men and women in the USA – and many Western cultures – in her 2020 music video 'The Man'. Convincingly dressed as a man and depicted living a playboy lifestyle, she calls out white male privilege. However, there are matriarchal societies around the world where this is not the case. Looking at such societies in different times and places proves that gender is a societal construct specific to particular cultures and eras.

Taylor Swift in her male disguise.

The Minangkabau in Indonesia

The Minangkabau ethnic group, indigenous to the highlands of West Sumatra, is one of the world's largest matrilineal societies. Ancestral property is inherited by daughters, children adopt their mother's name, and the Minang groom moves into the wife's ancestral home. As the heads of household and controllers of land and property, women arbitrate and resolve disputes in partnership with men, and play a crucial role in the community.

Minangkabau women in traditional ceremonial costume.

Social privilege theory: a theory that unpacks how power structures in society advantage certain privileged groups, often as a result of gender, race, nationality, disability, sexual orientation or religion.

The Queendom of Nubia

The great African queendom of Kush in Nubia was a historical rival for ancient Egypt. Lying along the Nile in what is now Ethiopia, Sudan and parts of Egypt, Kush was ruled by a series of warrior queens known as *kandake*. Practices of matrilineal succession meant that the right to rule passed down the women of the royal family. In this matriarchal queendom, queens were the heads, while kings (their brothers or sons, not their husbands) served as executive deputies, without authority to make decisions on their own. Throughout Nubia, the cult of Isis (the Egyptian goddess of healing and magical powers) had a tremendous following.

One of the most renowned *kandake* rulers was Amanirenas, who reigned during 40–10BCE (a similar period to Cleopatra). She led a victorious defeat over the Roman Empire after Caesar defeated Egypt and then attempted annexation of Nubia. She eventually brokered a favourable peace treaty with Rome, and the Nubian queendom prospered for another 400 years.

This illustration imagines a procession in the Queendom of Kush.

A *Mosuo woman hoes her field near Lugu Lake on the Yunnan plateau.*

'The Kingdom of Women'

The Mosuo are an ethnic group who live in Yunnan, south-west China, in the foothills of the Tibetan Himalayas. In what is dubbed the 'Kingdom of Women', women own and inherit property, work in the fields and run the households. Women and men practise *tisese* or 'walking marriages' – a term that means 'go back and forth' – whereby women can invite men to their private sleeping quarters, be it for one-night stands or long-term partnerships, which may or may not lead to pregnancy. In these sexual relations, there are no obligations. Women and men can change partners and experience sexuality with as many, or as few, people as they wish, free from judgement and the double standard that regulates women's sexuality in many cultures. Couples do not live together or marry, and extended families of both men and women bring up the children. This kinship structure provides women with equality and agency over their sexual and procreative lives.

The BriBri

The BriBri form one of the oldest matriarchal societies in the world and live in the mountainous region of Talamanca, Costa Rica. This indigenous matriarchal society is built on a matrilineal clan system, whereby women are the heads of family and hold ownership of and inherit land. Women and men often perform similar jobs, but some roles are gender specific, with women culturally venerated. Only women can prepare the sacred cacao drink used for spiritual ceremonies, whereas both women and men can be *awa* shamans. While there is at times a gendered division of labour, male and female roles are recognized as complementary and there is no status competition between the sexes.

A *Bribri woman making cacao in the traditional manner in the Talamanca region of Costa Rica.*

EGALITARIANISM, SISTER-BASED SOCIETIES OR MATRIARCHIES?

There is a diversity of gender relations around the world that cannot be reduced to Western ideas of total female or male supremacy. Comparative vocabularies like 'matriarchies' are helpful. However, trying to fit gender relations into a box – or seeing matriarchies as mirror images of patriarchies – can limit our understanding of the many ways that societies are structured. There are numerous societies studied by gender researchers (such as the Crow Native Americans, the Trobriand Islanders, the Lahu and Na of southern China, the Vanatinai of Sudest Island and the Tetum of Timor) that emphasize maternal symbols and complementarity of decision-making. They could be considered matriarchies, although they are all quite different from each other. Often existing in smaller societies, neither men nor women hold overarching authority, but share power and responsibilities as part of a gender parity.

The mighty women of Africa's medieval golden age

During the period prior to the brutalities of European colonization from the 17th century, Africa was the seat of a number of powerful and prosperous states. Trading centres such as Timbuktu and Djenne in West Africa, rich with salt and gold, became economic powerhouses and important hubs of culture and learning. Once-major African powers such as the kingdom of Mali, the Christian kingdom of Ethiopia or the city-state of Ife in Nigeria were cosmopolitan sites of exchange for goods, ideas, innovations and religious conceptions. The continent held a global reputation, from China to Europe, with rulers like Mansa Musa of the kingdom of Mali (r. 1312–37) being one of the richest individuals in the world.

Women were involved in the economy from the earliest times, participating in local and long-distance trading activities. Though many African settlements were more commonly led by men, women played a central role in societies, as business entrepreneurs and market traders, spiritual leaders, revered singers, mothers, rulers and for their part in sustaining communities.

Queen Amina, the Nigerian warrior

The legendary West African ruler Queen Amina (1533–1610) was a queen in the northern Nigerian Hausa state of Zazzau. She trained as a warrior, gaining notoriety and numerous accolades for her fierce military skills. Her abilities and reputation enabled her to become queen after her brother's death in what was a male-dominated society. According to legend, Amina would take a husband after every battle, spend a night with him and then execute him in the morning. Under Amina, the Zazzau state dramatically expanded to its largest territorial boundaries in history, with a vibrant trading network along east–west routes. To mark and protect these lands, Amina erected strong earthen walls around her cities, which became the prototype for fortifications used across Hausa states. Many have survived and are known as *ganuwar* Amina (Amina's walls). Amina herself remains culturally revered.

A modern representation of Queen Amina.

Early information on individual African women is well chronicled in Ethiopia, which was the centre of ancient Coptic Christianity. The Queen of Sheba, Makeda was the founding ruler of Ethiopia in the 10th century BCE. She is best known for testing King Solomon with clever riddles to prove his legitimacy to rule. The lineage of Queen Sheba lives on today. Queen Shebah III (1963–present) is the descendent of the oldest matriarchal throne in Africa and heads the African Kingdoms Federation.

Queen Lúwo Gbàgìdá

The traditional heartland of the Yoruba people is what is now Nigeria, Benin and Togo. Royal genealogies of Yoruba city-states detail several powerful female rulers. One such is Queen Lúwo Gbàgìdá (10th century), who reigned as the Ooni of Ife (an ancient Yoruba city-state in south-western Nigeria) and the supreme ruler of Yoruba land. Allegedly, she hated walking on bare earth so she pioneered baked clay tile pavements across the region.

The Mali empire (1240–1645)

Mali thrived as a dominant power in West Africa during the 13th to 17th centuries, the empire having been founded by Sundiata Keita following his victory over the Sosso Ghanaian empire. Under Mansa Musa, the ninth *mansa* (sultan) of the empire, Mali flourished as a result of the region's staggering wealth and control of crucial trade routes. The empire spread across modern-day Mali, Senegal, Gambia, Niger, Guinea, Nigeria, Chad, Burkina Faso and Mauritania. Mansa Musa brought architects from across Africa and the Middle East to design innovative new buildings for cosmopolitan cities like Timbuktu and Gao.

Queen Luwo of the Yoruba.

Tuareg women dressed for a marriage ceremony with traditional face paint.

Pastoral societies: the Tuareg

Societies that focus on herding animals, such as cattle, sheep, goats and camels, often involving migration to find good pasture, are called pastoral. Women have long played important roles in pastoral societies from the Tuareg and Fulani of the western Sahara through to the Masai of Kenya and Tanzania.

Among the nomadic Tuareg of Niger, women control livestock – a crucial source of wealth that is passed down through the female line – and hold positions of authority. The Tuareg long ago adopted Islamic religious practices, but with many unique twists. For instance, women do not wear the veil, whereas most men do, usually concealing their faces except for their eyes. Pre-marital sex is not seen as taboo and women can have as many sexual partners as they like. If they marry, women do not relinquish control, and still own their cattle and tent.

The great Mali Empire held enormous wealth, which is still evident today in the kingdom's monumental mud-based architecture, such as that of the Great Mosque at Djenne. Located on the flood plain of the Bani River, a mosque was first built there in the 13th century; the current building was constructed in 1907.

MUSICAL HISTORIANS

Few African societies of the Middle Ages, such as the Mali Empire, kept written archives. That said, a number of ancient African societies produced innovative writing systems and written texts, including Ge'ez (in Eritrea and Ethiopia), Punic and Libyco-Berber (in the Maghreb and Sahara), ancient Egyptian, Latin, Greek and Arabic. However, in many regions, oral transmission was prioritized over the written word and passed down through the generations. In West Africa, griots or *jeliw* are to this day crucial historians who chronicle and transmit historical knowledge through song, poetry and stories. Women singers or *jelimusow* are key parts of these hereditary oral traditions. Although they are generally limited to the public performance of historical epics, many enjoy immense popularity and are custodians of medieval histories.

Kandia Kouyate is a celebrated Malian jelimusow who continues the ancient tradition of chronicling West African history through song.

Tin Hinan (meaning 'she of the tents') was the Tuareg founding queen who reigned in the fourth century CE. Her monumental tomb is in the Hoggar Mountains of southern Algeria.

Polygamy and polyandry

Many patrilineal African societies have long practised polygyny or the custom of men having multiple wives, depending on the man's status. Reasons for this have been pinned to conservative Islamic interpretations but also to the development of agriculture. Having multiple wives meant a larger pool of labour and potentially more offspring to ensure the family's growth and success. Allowing only men to have multiple spouses is unequal, but the practice itself is not necessarily problematic, and in fact sometimes logical. There are instances of wives advocating for co-wives, as well as encouraging their sisters or cousins to be co-wives to share the burdens of farm work and child raising.

Less documented is the practice of polyandry, whereby a woman has multiple husbands or recognized lovers. Among the Birom in northern Nigeria, the practice of *njem* is a system that enables married women to have formally acknowledged relationships with men other than their husbands. Women can choose their additional partners, who mutually support one another.

Other systems have existed, too. Among the Yoruba, a widow who wanted to remain with her in-laws could marry a female relative. For the Nandi of Kenya, an older woman could marry a younger woman to look after her and have children for her, who would carry on the family lineage and inherit her wealth. Woman-to-woman marriages are also documented among the Fon, the Kikuyu and the Nuer, among others.

THE RAIN QUEEN

The Balobedu of South Africa's northern Limpopo province have, since the early 1800s, been ruled by a female monarch, the Rain Queen. These monarchs are believed to have the magical powers of bringing rain to the parched country. The position is inherited matrilineally and is one of only a handful of tribal monarchs officially recognized by the South African state. Traditionally, Rain Queens received gifts from their subjects, including their daughters as wives. Sometimes these wives were then paired with royal men to build alliances. The Rain Queen still holds great influence today. For instance, in popular culture, the fictional Marvel comics character Storm is written as a descendent of the Rain Queen dynasty.

This photograph by the Nigerian photographer Yagazie Emezi speaks to historical practices of same-sex marriages in Igboland, Nigeria. In some cases, women could choose more than one wife. All traditional marriage rites would be followed. European colonists attempted to stamp out many of these logical – and potentially liberatory – customs. It is ironical that Western countries often uphold themselves as the progressive ones and try to claim that feminism or LGBTQ+ rights are Western projects.

Colonialism and suppression

In pre-colonial times, women held powerful roles as monarchs, chieftains, queen mothers/sisters, priestesses, princesses, warriors, political figures and central economic players in long-distance trade. Under the brutality of colonialism, when European powers violently occupied some wealthy African regions, many of these diverse and progressive practices were suppressed. Instead, in many instances, people were encouraged to conform to European gender norms and divisions of labour. Customs such as same-sex marriages and matriarchal systems were depicted as primitive and heathen by missionaries and colonialists. Negotiations were often only conducted with titled men, contributing to the marginalization of African women from power.

Queen mothers are powerful leaders among many African ethnic groups. They have influential roles in local government, particularly among the Akan in the Ashanti kingdom of modern-day Ghana. Among the Akan, queen mothers rule alongside the chief or king, can appoint their own ministers, and hold veto power in decision making. With colonialism, their authority diminished, but since the 21st century, many queen mothers have regained influence.

Warrior women

The Middle Ages references a Western-centric view of history, but it was a significant period for many regions around the world. Without a system of geopolitically marked nation states, conflicts often erupted, with efforts to assert and expand ever-changing political borders, spread extremities of religious faith and claim resource-rich regions. Historical accounts all too frequently erase the role of women in medieval warfare from record. However, there are numerous examples of women during the Middle Ages who took up arms or commanded entire armies: sometimes in defence and sometimes with aggression. Women also played crucial roles on the home front, which is often neglected in favour of depictions of warfare as synonymous with combat.

Jennifer Lawrence's character Katniss Everdeen in the popular novel and film series The Hunger Games *is celebrated as a radical female hero who does not glorify or shy away from conflict. She inhabits both traditionally masculine and feminine roles as a warrior, sister, daughter, friend and romantic partner, who also battles with the mental health challenges of combat.*

Female knights in the Middle Ages

Women could not generally be granted the title of knight. However, there were still many women who were to all intents and purposes knights, except in name. Various chivalric orders of knighthood admitted women, such as the Knights Templar and the Teutonic Order. In Catalonia, Spain, the Order of the Hatchet was founded by the count of Barcelona to honour a group of women who defended the town of Tortosa against an attack by the Moors. There are also numerous examples of women of all classes who donned armour, directed troop movements and rode into war.

Marguerite d'Anjou (1430–82), Queen of England, ruled the kingdom in the place of her husband King Henry VI, who was frequently unwell. She was a principal figure during the civil wars known as the Wars of the Roses (1455–87), personally directing Lancastrian commanders in battles against Yorkist opponents.

Khawlah bint al-Azwar

Khawlah bint al-Azwar (b. 600s CE) was a leading Muslim commander and Companion of the Islamic Prophet Muhammad in the seventh century. She led Muslim troops during a series of early Islamic conquests in what is now Jordan, Syria and Palestine. In 636, she defeated the chief commander of the Byzantine army at the Battle of the Yarmuk, in which she led a troop of women against the Byzantine empire.

JOAN OF ARC

Joan of Arc (1412–31) is one of the most famous female warriors from the Middle Ages. Born to a peasant family in rural north-east France, Joan was a teenager when she received visions of saints telling her to expel the occupying English forces from France. These divine revelations drove her to offer her assistance to the military of France's King Charles VII during the Hundred Years' War (1337–1453). Although she was initially ridiculed, her efforts were taken seriously after her military strategizing paved the way for the French victory. Joan herself was captured by the Burgundians, French nobles allied with England. Despite escape attempts and rescue efforts, she was convicted of heresy and cross-dressing by the English and burned alive at the stake in 1431, at just 19 years of age. More than 460 years later, Pope Benedict XV declared Joan a saint. Her strategies are said to have greatly influenced French battle tactics.

The hidden history of female samurai warriors

Women samurai warriors in Japan have a long history, dating back
to 200CE when Empress Jingū took the throne and led an invasion of
Silla (modern-day Korea). The *onna-bugeisha* were members of the *bushi*
noble samurai class in feudal Japan. They were trained in the art of
warfare and martial arts to defend their communities against enemy
warriors. From the 12th to 17th centuries, female samurai warriors
were hugely popular across Japan and fought battles on every front.
However, the Edo period from the 17th century shifted the status
of women in Japanese society. Neo-Confucian philosophy began to
dominate, altering the acceptability of warrior culture. For women,
this meant a growing expectation of domesticity and maternal life. The
Battle of Aizu (1868) is generally considered to be the final stand of
the *onna-bugeisha*, during which the legendary female samurai Nakano
Takeko (1847–68) led a group of female samurai – known as the *joshitai*
– against the emperor's forces.

*Western popular culture has rewritten the history of
Japanese warring culture to depict samurai warriors
as men, when this was far from the case.*

Tomoe Gozen (late 12th century) is one of the most famous female samurai in Japanese history. In the medieval chronicle of the Genpei War, the *Heike Monogatari*, she is described as 'a fearless rider whom neither the fiercest horse nor the roughest ground could dismay, and so dexterously did she handle sword and bow that she was a match for a thousand warriors'. Her expert talents included horseback riding, archery and the art of the *katana* sword used by samurai. She was known as *onna-musha* because she engaged in offensive battle rather than defensive fighting associated with *onna-bugeisha*. The centuries that came after Tomoe Gozen were the golden age for the *onna-bugeisha* and *onna-musha*. They made up a large part of the samurai class, protected villages across the Japanese empire, and opened schools to train young women in military strategy and martial arts.

Tomoe Gozen killing Uchida Saburo Ieyoshi at the Battle of Awazu no Hara c.1750.

Were the Amazons real?

The Amazons of ancient Greek mythology were fierce warrior women said to roam Scythia, a vast area surrounding the Black Sea stretching from eastern Europe across Siberia and all the way to Mongolia. The Amazons were known among the Greeks as beautiful and deadly, as well as courageous and skilled in warfare.

First documented by the poet Homer in the *Iliad* in the eighth century BCE, thrilling tales of the bloodthirsty Amazons were popular in Greek society. Greek artists created images of Amazons wearing trousers, shooting bows, hurling spears, riding horses and fighting and dying heroically. Evocative scenes of warrior women in battle covered temples and buildings: a stark counterpoint to the patriarchal system that Greek women navigated.

Modern historians long assumed the Amazons to be fantastical myths. But since the 1940s, archaeologists studying Scythian sites in southern Russia, Ukraine, Caucasia and Central Asia have repeatedly unearthed hundreds of ancient female skeletons in grave mounds or *kurgans* filled with spears, axes, arrows and horses. These match those depicted in ancient Greek artwork of the Amazons, confirming the belief that the Amazons were indeed real and drawn from Scythian equestrian nomads – fierce warlike tribes who roamed the steppes of Siberia between 200 and 900BCE and whose lives centred around horses and archery; they were in fact the first people to domesticate and ride horses. Further research into Scythian culture reveals a gender egalitarianism. Both girls and boys learned how to ride and shoot from a young age, to hunt and defend the tribe. Regardless of gender, Scythians all dressed in practical tunics and trousers. They were so feared that the Chinese went to the extreme of building an entire fortress wall – the Great Wall of China – to keep them out!

A Greek soldier fighting an Amazon warrior. The Amazons were depicted by the Greeks as mythical warrior women who cut off their breasts to better draw their bows and murdered their male children. Some modern historians interpret these portrayals of barbarian women as a means of reinforcing ancient Greek patriarchy: after all, 'look what happens when women have too much power'! Others see Amazonian mythology as a liberatory space where gender fluidity could be explored within societal conventions.

'FIGHTS AS WELL AS A MAN'?

When Homer first described the Amazons in the *Iliad*, he referred to them as 'the equals of men'. Statements like this or ones such as 'fights as well as a man' are common in discussions around female athleticism. It reveals how entrenched the erroneous notion of male superiority can be in some cultures. According to this train of thought, strength is associated with masculine characteristics, communicating the misguided belief that strength and weakness are essential parts of one's sex or gender.

Some tribes and ethnic groups from Central Asia have long led egalitarian lifestyles in which women and men contributed to defence, war efforts and hunting. Many of the warriors in Genghis Khan's Mongol empire (on the other side of the Eurasian Steppe to Scythia) were women. In Mongolia today, women are prominent archers and equestrians.

The World Turned Upside Down *is an inverted conception of gender roles in medieval European society, but human cultural inventions of gender vary across different times and places.*

Chapter
3 GENDER AND DIVISIONS OF LABOUR

In this print, *The World Turned Upside Down*, by the medieval German printmaker Israhel Van Meckenem the Younger (1442–1503), gender roles are allegedly reversed. A woman holds a sceptre, symbolizing power and authority, while a man is spinning on a loom. However, Meckenem's depiction is not of an inverted global reality, but one that was culturally and historically contingent to his particular location and era, and even social class. As we have seen in previous chapters, women might not have been the powerholders in many patriarchal societies, but they certainly were in some regions of the world, making Meckenem's depiction hardly outlandish.

Gender roles around the world

There is nothing innate about being a 'woman' or 'man' that universally prescribes one to particular tasks – such as weaving or politics – or ranks these tasks hierarchically. For example, in the Inca empire of the Andes, both men and women produced textiles, whereas among the Navajo Native Americans, male weavers have always been part of traditional cultural practices. Gender egalitarianism is also a core cultural value in a number of ethnic groups around the world, defined by equal power and prestige. By looking at examples of gender role variations and the lives of women in different regions of the world, we can see just how much divisions of labour both vary and also have important similarities in diverse cultural and historical contexts.

Man's work? In some cultures, leadership, assertiveness and involvement in business or politics are stereotypically associated with the male child. However, what is viewed as 'man's work' in one society is 'woman's work' in another, or sometimes not even neatly partitioned into this kind of gender-binary divide.

Gender roles vary tremendously in different regions of the world. In fact, social scientists have long pointed to these variations to show how gender and sexuality are not natural but invented by humans. Gender and sexuality are deeply embedded in cultural practices and take on diverse meanings in different times and places. In many Western countries, women have for centuries been associated with domestic, 'light' tasks and nurturing behaviour, whereas men are connected to heavy labour, strength, dominance and aggression. However, in many places, this is far from the case. Biology does not prescribe the roles that men and women play. Even though we are often taught to think of our sex, gender and sexuality as natural, these roles are culturally constructed, learned and alterable categories.

Amanda Smith was an engineer at the Douglas Aircraft factory in southern California during World War II.

While every culture has in some way institutionalized the roles of men and women, it has not necessarily been in terms of contrasts between the prescribed personalities of the two sexes, nor in terms of dominance or submission.
– Margaret Mead, *Sex and Gender* (1935)

Margaret Mead is shown here 'conducting' Arapesh men who are playing secular flutes. In contrast to sacred flutes, from which women and children must hide, women were allowed to see these flutes.

Margaret Mead

Margaret Mead (1901–79) was a pioneering American anthropologist who showed that patterns of male and female behaviour differ greatly across cultures through her research with the Arapesh, Mundugumor and Tchambuli of Papua New Guinea. Mead compared the differing gender roles among each ethnic group with gender role expectations in the USA. She argued that socialization shaped differing views of sexuality, including behaviour that had previously been seen as biological in origin. Mead used this evidence to call for changes in parenting and education in the USA.

The Tchambuli

The Tchambuli (now Chambri) of Papua New Guinea are an ethnic group in the Chambri Lakes region of Papua New Guinea. Traditionally, women are the primary suppliers of food and carry out business transactions. They fish for the community and travel to trade the surplus in surrounding markets. Men, on the other hand, take on roles in political arenas and are involved in ceremonial events. Since Mead's research, anthropologists have disputed her theories of Chambri female dominance. Nevertheless, the role of women in Chambri food gathering and bartering shows how sexual divisions of labour based on gender roles are socially constructed and have no basis in biology.

ABOVE: *Tchambuli (Chambri) children adorned in traditional body paint.*

The Dahomey Amazons

From the 17th to 19th centuries, women served as soldiers for the Kingdom of Dahomey's army in what is now Benin. Dubbed the 'Dahomey Amazons', these frontline soldiers and bodyguards were known for their fearlessness and strength. Part of the reason for the ascendance of women in the military was because of the loss of men, who were captured and forcibly shipped from Dahomey during the brutal European slave trade. Another crucial element was the recognition that individuals can be skilful in all manner of practices, such as armed combat, regardless of gender. Many female Dahomey soldiers became advocates in their communities and still play important ceremonial roles.

The Dahomey Amazons pictured in 1897.

Gender stereotypes

Gender stereotypes are so powerful because gender is heavily emphasized in many cultural practices around the world. At a young age, children often learn clear expectations for girls and boys. When they do not conform to culturally appropriate gender roles, they may face societal policing such as criticism, bullying, marginalization or rejection by family, teachers and peers. Girls and boys can be subject to extreme ridicule for gender nonconformity. For example, boys can be under a lot of pressure to repress their emotions. Once we become adults, gender roles are a firm aspect of our personalities, and we often hold gender stereotypes around what is 'acceptable'.

In many Western cultures, men outnumber women in such professions as military, law enforcement and politics. Women, on the other hand, outnumber men in care-related occupations including social work, nursing and childcare. These occupational gender roles are derived from Western cultural traditions. They can affect what an individual perceives as obtainable and the social pressures they experience, but do not necessarily reflect an individual's personal preference.

Even at a very young age, children are expected to fulfil specific gender roles.

Beyond the gender binary

Not all cultures divide humans into only two genders. In some cultures, gender is much more fluid. An individual could be born as one biologic sex but then take on another gender or have the option of more than two genders to select.

ABOVE: *Brotherboys and Sistergirls are Aboriginal and Torres Strait Islander people who were assigned one sex at birth, but live their lives through a different gender spirit. Mistaken Western framings as gay or trans do not encompasses the unique cultural identity of this non-binary gender diversity.*

LEFT: *The soccer player Abby Wambach (b. 1980) is a sports icon, FIFA Women's World Cup Champion and two-time Olympic gold medallist who has defied gender expectations around what sports are 'appropriate' for girls versus boys. Even so, Wambach received significantly lower pay than her male soccer counterparts. She has talked openly about her financial struggles after retiring from the field and has since been a vocal advocate for gender equality and closing the pay gap.*

Female construction workers

Whether engaged in digging ditches, thatching roofs or masonry or carpentry, women have long been involved in the construction industry. However, today, they often represent just a fraction of the construction industry workforce, although that number is steadily increasing. In the UK, the architect Holly Porter created the networking organization 'Chicks with Bricks' to support women forging careers in the British construction industry.

A woman engineer supervising a construction site.

In many regions of India, women make up a substantial part of construction workforces. However, they are often far less recognized than their male counterparts, receive much lower pay, face limitations on their selection for skilled jobs and promotions, and are subject to sexual harassment. The majority of female constructions workers come from lower socio-economic backgrounds and are prevented from advancing into higher-paid jobs. Like 'Chicks with Bricks', organizations such as the Self Employed Women's Association (SEWA), India's largest female trade union, focus on advocating for the rights of female labourers, including training and certification.

Female construction workers in India balancing bricks on their heads.

Motherhood and the politics of domestic work

Motherhood is one of the foremost instruments traditionally used to dominate and domesticate women. However, cross-cultural understandings also challenge another central stereotype surrounding gender roles: the 'burden' of pregnancy and child-rearing. There is the biological component of female conception, which can shape gender roles – although even this is no longer necessary with scientific advances. In cases where women take on the reproductive role, this does not prevent them from doing other jobs. In some cultures, women might engage more in work that is seen as compatible with reproductive and child-rearing roles, such as cooking and managing the household. In others, parenting is distributed co-operatively and gender roles are more fluid.

The cult of domesticity

During the Victorian era of the 19th century, many upper- and middle-class American and European women were heavily regulated by the system known as 'the cult of domesticity'. This emphasized that a woman's role was within the home and that their responsibilities were to the family. According to this notion, the 'ideal' woman should maintain the four virtues of piety, purity, domesticity and submissiveness. Missionaries and colonial authorities attempted to export this system around the world under the mantra of 'civilization'. These normative ideas of gender roles have had a powerful influence in shaping diverse conceptions of gender around the world.

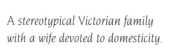
A stereotypical Victorian family with a wife devoted to domesticity.

The American poet, essayist and feminist Adrienne Rich (1929–2012) made an important distinction between motherhood as a patriarchal institution and mothering as a woman's relationship to her powers of reproduction and children. Motherhood studies have since examined motherhood as a phenomenon that is mythologized through hegemonic constructions of 'ideal mothers', 'natural mothers' and 'maternal instincts'. Instead, we should see motherhood as enacted in many diverse ways.

A classic image from a 1950s cooker advertisement shows a 'perfect housewife' mother preparing delicious food for her husband and children.

What is an 'ideal mother'?

Consider how the model of the 1950s white American housewife is a hegemonic construct, meaning that it is a cultural invention that exerts huge social, cultural, ideological and economic influence. In reality, this is a romanticized conception of motherhood that reproduces patriarchal stereotypes. This ideal of femininity also excludes women of colour and those of lower socio-economic backgrounds.

Co-parenting cultures: Aka men in central/west Africa play a crucial role in child-rearing without stigmatization surrounding father–child intimacy. This is not to say that everything is egalitarian – men invariably hold the top leadership positions. However, gender roles are fluid when it comes to hunting and co-caring in the parenting sphere.

'SITTING THE MOON'
坐月子

Zuo yue zi or 'sitting the moon' is a Chinese post-partum practice dating back to the 10th century. After the birth of their child, the mother will 'sit for a month'. Relatives will take care of them, preparing special nourishing foods and herbal treatments. Traditionally, zuo yue zi involved following strict rules, such as not going outside, showering or drinking cold water as part of the beliefs surrounding the physical and emotional recuperation required after childbirth. Zuo yue zi is still widely practised today, although often in ways that are more compatible with contemporary contexts, including hiring live-in assistants.

Childcare in many regions of the world is generally not the responsibility of the birth mother alone, but is rather taken on by multiple caregivers, such as partners, relatives, neighbours and siblings. In some cultures, such as among the Nso in Cameroon, is it thought that children should not develop exclusive attachments to their mothers, but cultivate equally close bonds with siblings, neighbours and other members of the community.

Among the Aka of the present-day Central African Republic, fathers have crucial intimate roles with newborn infants. There is still a sexual division of labour in that women are the primary caregivers, but there is a flexibility whereby men and women's roles are interchangeable as needed. While women hunt, men will look after the children; while men cook, women will decide on the next camp, and vice versa.

One of the deepest stereotypes of motherhood is that mothers are apolitical and isolated with their children from social struggles. This image extends from what the historian Annelise Orleck calls the 'mutually absorbed madonna and child'. Mothers have been involved in concerted activism, taking advantage of the politics of motherhood to address survival needs of their communities and children. The Mothers of the Plaza de Mayo in Argentina are one group well known for their strategizing and using images of motherhood strategically without appearing threatening, even as they place themselves in danger in the performance of motherhood.

LEFT: *Motherhood as resistance: The Mothers of the Plaza de Mayo was formed in 1977 in Argentina with the goal of finding the children who had been forcibly 'disappeared' (the* desaparecidos) *under the military dictatorship of Jorge Rafael Videla. During the 'Dirty War' (1973–83), as many as 30,000 people were kidnapped and killed under alleged charges of political dissidence. To draw attention to the military junta's actions, the mothers wore babies' diapers as headscarves during their weekly demonstrations at the Plaza, which they embroidered with the names of their children.*

Reproductive labour

The Italian academic-activist Silvia Federici (b. 1942) has long argued that domestic work is unpaid labour that is rendered invisible. Federici was the founder of the Wages for Housework movement in the 1970s, critiquing how capitalist societies do not acknowledge or support 'reproductive labour'.

The labour question has challenged many mainstream feminists, who have also rejected domestic labour in favour of measuring women's empowerment by their influence in other workplaces. However, this overlooks that for some women, caring for their children and households full-time is a personal preference that should not be dismissed as a form of patriarchal enslavement. It also disregards that not engaging in reproductive labour is sometimes achieved by outsourcing domestic work and childcare to less economically advantaged women for low wages.

Federici and others have pushed back against some mainstream feminists to value all work that women do that is rendered invisible by the capitalist patriarchy. Statistics show that the majority of childcare and household responsibilities fall on women even when they have full-time jobs in formal labour forces. The American sociologist Arlie Hochschild coined the term 'the second shift' to describe this labour performed at home in addition to paid work. These arguments resurged during the COVID-19 pandemic as many women, in particular, faced juggling multiple jobs as wage earners, care workers and educators. Recently, housework has been made more visible, but it still is not given monetary compensation as work that underpins the economy.

Workplace policies have historically made it very difficult for women to advance in the workplace and have a family, including requiring women to quit their jobs if they get pregnant or married.

The Italian feminist writer Silvia Federici, who coined the term 'reproductive labour'.

Reproductive labour – a term used by Silvia Federici and other feminist thinkers to describe all the continuous sustaining work we do to enable ourselves and those around us to thrive. This could be making breakfast in the morning or helping an elderly relative. It is work disregarded by our economic system.

Many employers have started to address these issues by offering on-site breastfeeding facilities and childcare and parental and adoption leave. Finland has some of the most generous parental leave policies in the world for caregivers regardless of gender: 164 days of paid leave for each parent, 69 of which can be transferred to the other parent. This are not surprising in Finland. In 1906, it was the the second country in the world to give women the right to vote, after New Zealand in 1893. In 2019, Finland went on to elect the world's youngest prime minister (aged 34 at the time), Sanna Marin, who headed a predominantly female cabinet with 12 out of the 18 ministers being women.

Imagine if women around the world stopped doing the domestic, unpaid labour they carry out every day, such as cooking, cleaning, laundry, childcare and shopping. The global economy would collapse!

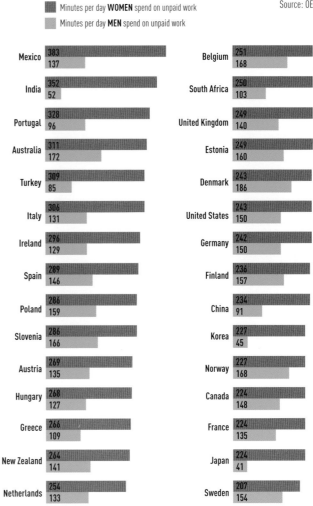

Source: OECD

Legend:
- ■ Minutes per day **WOMEN** spend on unpaid work
- ■ Minutes per day **MEN** spend on unpaid work

Country	Women	Men
Mexico	383	137
India	352	52
Portugal	328	96
Australia	311	172
Turkey	309	85
Italy	306	131
Ireland	296	129
Spain	289	146
Poland	286	159
Slovenia	286	166
Austria	269	135
Hungary	268	127
Greece	266	109
New Zealand	264	141
Netherlands	254	133
Belgium	251	168
South Africa	250	103
United Kingdom	249	140
Estonia	249	160
Denmark	243	186
United States	243	150
Germany	242	150
Finland	236	157
China	234	91
Korea	227	45
Norway	227	168
Canada	224	148
France	224	135
Japan	224	41
Sweden	207	154

Comparison between the unpaid work that women and men do in a range of different countries c.2019.

In 2022, the leaders of four of the five parties of Finland's governing coalition were women.

Arrangements like Finland's equal parental leave policies look to promote gender equality.

THE NOTORIOUS RBG: A TRAILBLAZER FOR GENDER EQUALITY

Throughout her distinguished career, Ruth Bader Ginsburg (1933–2020), Supreme Court Justice and co-founder of the American Civil Liberties Union (ACLU) Women's Rights Project, was a pioneer for gender equality. Ginsburg studied law at Harvard: one of only nine women to do so in 1956 in a class of around 500 men. At the time, the law school dean asked her and her female classmates why they were taking seats that could be filled by men.

Ginsburg persevered, finishing her studies at Columbia Law School, New York City at the top of her class. Despite being recommended for a clerkship with Supreme Court Justice Felix Frankfurter, she was pushed back with the response that she was not a man. Ginsburg experienced continued discrimination both as a practising lawyer and in academia at Rutgers Law School, New Jersey, where she discovered her salary was lower than that of her male colleagues. Together with other female faculty members, she joined an equal pay campaign that led to substantial increases in pay for female professors.

These experiences prompted Ginsburg to take on sex discrimination complaints sent to her by the ACLU. She co-founded the ACLU Women's Rights Project (WRP) with Brenda Feigen (b. 1944) in 1972 to removal artificial barriers of discrimination for women, men and non-binary individuals. In the same year, she became the first woman at Columbia Law School to be granted tenure.

Many of the cases Ginsburg took on were focused on supporting all people to thrive regardless of gender. This was best shown in the 1970s in the case of Charles Moritz. Moritz held sole responsibility for care of his elderly mother but had been denied a tax deduction for caregiving because he was an unmarried man. Ginsburg showed the male judges that sex discrimination hurts men as much as women. In their defence, the government made a lengthy list of federal statutes that distinguished between women and men, arguing that if Ginsburg was right, all these hundreds of other laws would also be unconstitutional. Rather than backing down, the list ('Appendix E') became the playbook for the WRP in systematically targeting every single

I Dissent!
Ginsburg was famous for her jazzy 'dissent' collars, which she wore when she gave powerful opinions at odds with the conservative majority of the Supreme Court. Her distinctive collars speak to what she called 'the dissenter's hope' in 'writing not for today but for tomorrow'. Ginsburg attracted a huge fan base among young liberals that continues to this day, earning her the nickname 'Notorious RBG' after the legendary rapper Notorious B.I.G..

Ginsburg had numerous impacts on people's lives in the USA, including ensuring:

- that men receive the same caregiving and Social Security rights as women (1971)

- protections for pregnant women in the workplace, including the inability to be fired from their jobs (1972)

- a woman's right to choose whether she gives birth (Roe v. Wade 1973)

- that women can apply for bank accounts, credit cards and mortgages without a male co-signer (1974)

- that employers cannot discriminate against employees based on gender or reproductive choices (1978)

- that juries must include women (1979)

- that state-sponsored educational institutions cannot exclude women on account of their gender (1996)

- strengthening equal pay protections

- a key vote in granting same-sex marriages (2015)

law that discriminated on the basis of sex. Since then, the WRP has continued to challenge employer policies in the USA that generalize women as the primary caregivers at home. Instead, they fight for women and men to receive equal benefits such as parental leave to allow for more equitable family roles.

Ginsburg's work was widely respected outside the ACLU. In 1980, she was appointed as a judge of the US Court of Appeals for the District of Columbia Circuit. Just over a decade later, President Bill Clinton appointed her to the Supreme Court in 1993. She became the second female justice on the Supreme Court. Known for her progressive votes on crucial issues, Ginsburg fought fiercely for affirmative action (efforts to improve educational, employment and other opportunities for people who have been previously subject to discrimination), same-sex marriage, abortion and healthcare.

Ginsburg's time on the Supreme Court was one of the most memorable in modern history. Few justices have the confidence to stand up for the rights of people who have been marginalized, including women, non-binary, LGBTQ+ and disabled people and Native Americans. Ginsburg would never go with the majority if she felt that an unjust decision had been made. Instead, she would dissent in a well-researched and highly articulate manner. She has had a lasting influence not only on the legal world but also as an example of a powerful woman who continues to energize younger generations.

Women in contemporary politics

More women are entering politics and governmental leadership at the highest levels than ever before. Many countries are implementing parliamentary quotas to guarantee a substantial representation of women. A number of countries and political parties employ a 'zipper system' to ensure gender equality in politics: parties create a candidate list that alternates between candidates of different genders for each seat a party wins. This can enable a near 50:50 split between the elected male and female candidates. Policies like this have progressed national political systems towards a significant global milestone, with over a quarter of women worldwide now in parliamentary positions. But women make up over half the world's population, meaning that these numbers are still not what they should be.

Degrees of representation

Worldwide, women remain under-represented in positions of leadership. Although the number of female heads of state has increased over the past two decades, women in government leadership are still a minority. Gender norms and expectations continue to impact the number of women who access government leadership positions. Women ministers are often assigned portfolios related to energy, the environment or social sectors, which largely excludes them from the executive branches of government.

PROPORTION OF WOMEN IN NATIONAL PARLIAMENTS (MARCH 2022)

1. Rwanda 61.3 per cent

2. Cuba 53.4 per cent

3. Nicaragua 50.6 per cent

4. Mexico and United Arab Emirates 50 per cent

5. New Zealand 49.2 per cent

Rwanda's gender equality

Rwanda is leading the way on female representation in politics: 61 per cent of parliamentary seats in the east-central African country are held by women. In the wake of Rwanda's devastating 1994 genocide, the government has focused on women's education and mandatory quotas of parliamentary seats for women.

Women MPs in Rwanda's parliament.

The Costa Rican system

Costa Rica has vertical and horizontal zipper system laws. This requires that political parties' candidates for the national legislature are half women and that parties must list female and male candidates in alternating order, rather than putting all male candidates first. Costa Rica is consistently in the top 10 countries for the highest percentage of women in national parliaments. But these zipper policies do not always address gender inequalities. In May 2022, the conservative economist Rodrigo Chaves took presidential office in Costa Rica, despite being found to have sexually harassed multiple women while employed at the World Bank. He promised to roll back sexual and reproductive rights, which could ultimately affect many women's access to leadership positions.

Speaking in the Costa Rican parliament.

The UAE

Sheikha Lubna bint Khalid bin Sultan Al Qasimi (b. 1962) was the first female minister of the United Arab Emirates (UAE). In the UAE, 50 per cent of parliamentary seats are held by women. Increased gender diversity in parliament is crucial, but it is only one step towards equality, particularly when restrictive laws remain in place. Emirati women are still subject to male guardian authority, leading some to question whether the female political quotas are merely tokenism.

The UAE's first woman minister, Sheika Lubna bint Kalid bin Sultan Al Qasimi.

New Zealand's political diversity

With Jacinda Ardern (b. 1980) as prime minister, New Zealand has the most diverse parliament in the world. Almost half of New Zealand's parliament members are women and 11 per cent are LGBTQ+. Indigenous M āori and Pacific Islanders are represented at a higher rate than in the overall population. Ardern herself made history as the youngest female leader of a country, aged 37 (although since superseded by Finland's Sanna Marin). She is famous around the world for her progressive policies.

Jacinda Ardern, youthful architect of New Zealand's forward-looking policy.

Legendary leadership milestones

The first woman to be elected democratically as a head of a government in the modern world was Prime Minister Sirimavo Bandaranaike (1916–2000) in 1960 in present-day Sri Lanka, then known as Ceylon. Bandaranaike played a trail-blazing role in the decolonization and state-building processes of the newly independent Sri Lanka. She served three terms: 1960–5, 1970–7 and 1994–2000. Her daughter, Chandrika Kumaratunga (b. 1945), served as Sri Lanka's prime minister and then its first woman president from 1994 to 2005.

Sirimavo Bandaranaike led Sri Lanka in three decades.

Vigdís Finnbogadóttir

Vigdís Finnbogadóttir (b. 1930) of Iceland was the first woman elected president of a country in 1980. Her election came at a time of huge strides in the Icelandic women's movement. During the 1975 International Women's Year, 90 per cent of Icelandic women went on strike to show how undervalued domestic work was. As part of the momentum for female leadership, Finnbogadóttir was encouraged to run against the other male candidates. She was hugely popular and was re-elected three times to become the longest-serving elected female head of state in history, with 16 years in office. She worked on promoting female education, environmental activism and Icelandic culture.

The very popular Vigdís Finnbogadóttir of Iceland.

Indira Gandhi

Indira Gandhi (1917–84) was the third prime minister of India and to date the country's only female prime minister, serving from 1966 until 1977 and then from 1980 until her assassination in 1984. Her father was Jawaharlal Nehru, India's first prime minister and one of the leaders of the country's independence movement. Gandhi gained widespread support for her agricultural improvements to India's self-sufficiency in food-grain production, known as the Green Revolution. She is legendarily known as India's great authoritarian. She increased India's influence so that it became the major regional power of South Asia, but also later instituted a controversial state-of-emergency policy whereby thousands of dissidents were imprisoned. In 1984, she violently suppressed an extremist uprising at the Golden Temple in Amritsar from Sikhs seeking an autonomous state. She was assassinated by her Sikh bodyguards in retaliation.

Indira Gandhi was a popular but divisive leader of India.

Margaret Thatcher

Margaret Thatcher (1925–2013) was prime minister of the UK from 1979 to 1990. She was the longest-serving British prime minister, re-elected twice, and the first woman to hold that position. Known as the 'Iron Lady', Thatcher was a controversial leader. She implemented policies known as 'Thatcherism', which included cutting social welfare programmes, the privatization of previously state-owned industries (gas, water and electricity) and the marginalization of trade unions. Infamously, she closed coal mines across the UK, while also reducing the power of labour organizers. She was eventually forced to resign during an internal leadership struggle after she tried to introduce an unpopular local poll tax.

Margaret Thatcher made over Britain's Conservative party along neoliberal lines, a legacy that lasted for decades.

Angela Merkel

Angela Merkel (b. 1954) was the chancellor of Germany from 2005 to 2021. Arguably one of the most powerful women in the world during her tenure, Merkel was described as the de facto leader of the European Union. She steered Germany through financial crisis into a period of unprecedented economic growth. Under Merkel, Germany rose as Europe's leading economic powerhouse, often spearheading bailout assistance to other financially struggling countries. She also advanced welcoming immigration policies, including providing resettlement opportunities for more than a million Syrians leaving their civil war – roughly 85 per cent of those seeking asylum in Europe at the time. During Merkel's leadership, more women were appointed into the German government than ever before. However, Germany has been slow to achieve full gender equity. Many women still face putting their careers on the back burner because of the tardy implementation of equal opportunity policies.

Angela Merkel was a stabilizing force in Europe during a turbulent era.

Tsai Ing-wen has pursued an outward-looking, progressive agenda during her terms in office.

Tsai Ing-wen

Tsai Ing-wen (b. 1956) became the first female president of Taiwan in 2016 and went on to be re-elected in 2020. She was the first person with ancestry in a Taiwanese ethnic minority (Hakka) to be elected to that office. Ing-wen was a legal academic and focused on asserting Taiwan's presence and stimulating the national economy to combat China's attempts at dominance. Few countries formally recognize Taiwan as a sovereign nation, but Ing-wen has played a key role in advancing its geopolitical relations and pushing the country to become one of East Asia's strongest democracies. She has focused on green energy and producing Taiwan's power from renewable sources, such as solar and wind, aiming to reach a net-zero emissions target by 2050. She also led Taiwan to become the first Asian country to legalize gay marriage. Her leadership during the COVID-19 pandemic was seen as a global model: Taiwan took early action to prevent the virus's spread and had neither significant case numbers nor the requirement for lockdown measures implemented by many other countries.

Mia Mottley

Mia Mottley (b. 1965) was elected the prime minister of Barbados in 2018. She oversaw its transition to a republic with the removal of the British monarch Queen Elizabeth II as the country's head of state. In stating that the country should abolish the constitutional monarchy after 54 years of independence, she argued powerfully for the importance of Barbados 'fully leaving [the] colonial past behind'. She grabbed headlines around the world for her campaigning against pollution, deforestation and climate change. Under Mottley's leadership, Barbados developed an ambitious plan for using solar power for electricity and phasing out fossil fuels. She is a vocal advocate for the impacts of climate change on small-island developing states.

Barbadian PM Mia Mottley, a persuasive voice for climate reform.

Pictured in a form of traditional dress, Hilaria Supa Huam has fought for indigenous rights in Peru.

Hilaria Supa Huam

Hilaria Supa Huamán (b. 1957) is an indigenous Peruvian politician who was elected to Peru's Congress in 2006. She experienced extreme sexism, racism and violence when working as a house maid, which left her with chronic health conditions and encouraged her political activism. She led protests against the forced sterilization of indigenous women and men, done under the dictatorship of Alberto Fujimori. Huamán was the first parliamentarian in Peru to take the oath to serve in an indigenous language; doing so in Quechua. She focuses on encouraging ancient Andean culture and advocating for poor indigenous communities and survivors of domestic and sexual abuse.

Michelle Bachelet

Michelle Bachelet (b. 1951) was the first female president of Chile (2006–10; 2014–18) and the first elected female president in South America. Her father was a general in the Chilean air force, who was arrested for opposing the dictator Augusto Pinochet's military coup. Bachelet, then a medical student, and her mother, an archaeologist, were both tortured and moved to Europe to escape. Becoming involved in Chilean politics after the end of the Pinochet regime, she is credited with seeing the country through the global financial crisis with astute economic planning, as well as reducing poverty and improving children's education. She has served as the United Nations High Commissioner for Human Rights since 2018.

Wangari Muta Maathai

Wangari Muta Maathai (1940–2011) was a Kenyan political activist, the first woman in East or Central Africa to earn a Ph.D., and in 2004 became the first African woman to receive the Nobel Peace Prize. While serving in the National Council of Women of Kenya, she developed the idea of community-based tree planting into a grassroots organization, the Green Belt Movement. This pioneering NGO encourages people, and particularly women, to plant trees to combat deforestation and environmental degradation. Maathai used her organization to focus on female empowerment by helping women set up their own tree-planting nurseries and having them take on leadership roles in community-based environmental projects. She was a member of parliament and served as assistant minister in the Ministry for Environmental and Natural Resources.

ABOVE: *Michelle Bachelet, two times president of Chile.*

RIGHT: *Kenyan activist Wangari Muta Maathai encouraged the planting of trees as a form of empowerment.*

Youthful senator Sarah McBride was the first transgender senator to work at the White House.

Sarah McBride

Sarah McBride (b. 1990) was the USA's first openly transgender state senator and the first to work at the White House. Elected in November 2020, McBride serves in the Delaware State Senate and is a leading public voice in America on LGBTQ+ equality. She pushed the Delaware state legislature to pass a law in 2013 that prohibited discrimination based on gender identity. Previously, a transgender person could be denied housing, fired from their job or even refused service at a restaurant with no legal protections. When discussing her election to the state senate, McBride said: 'It is my hope that a young LGBTQ kid here in Delaware or really anywhere in this country can look at the results and know that our democracy is big enough for them, too.'

Aung San Suu Kyi

Aung San Suu Kyi (b. 1945) is a Burmese politician and 1991 Nobel Peace Prize laureate. She was crucial in Myanmar's transition in the 2010s from military junta to democracy. She became a prominent figure in the People Power Uprising or 8888 Uprising of August 1988. Her party, the National League for Democracy (NLD), gained massive support in the nationwide protests against the totalitarian one-party military state. Despite her winning 81 per cent of seats in government in the 1990 elections, the military regime refused to recognize the results. Instead, Suu Kyi was placed under house arrest for 15 years between 1989 and 2010. In 2015, she led the NLD to a landslide victory in the country's first election in 25 years, and again in the 2020 elections. But in 2021 she was arrested once more following a military coup that sparked protests across the country. She is famous for her peaceful protests in the face of violent opposition. 'The Lady', as Suu Kyi is known, is still hugely popular among the country's Buddhist majority. However, once a beacon for human rights, she is now a controversial figure. She has been internationally condemned for complicity

Iconic but divisive Burmese politician Aung San Sui Kyi.

in the violence that led to hundreds of thousands of Rohingya Muslims from Myanmar seeking protection in neighbouring Bangladesh. She is also facing corruption cases, alleging that she accepted bribes, among other charges. While some argue that these are strategies to discredit her and justify the military's seizure of power, others are persuaded by Suu Kyi's fall from grace.

Supporting female leadership

Ellen Johnson Sirleaf (b. 1938), the 24th president of Liberia (2006–18), was the first woman to be elected head of state in a contemporary African country. She came to power after 14 years of brutal civil war in Liberia. Sirleaf rebuilt Liberia's essential infrastructure and brought in an economic revival that helped advance sustained peace in the country. In 2011, she was awarded the Nobel Peace Prize along with the Liberian activist Leymah Gbowee (b. 1972) and Yemen activist Tawakkol Karman (b. 1979). Since her presidency, Sirleaf has focused on supporting other African women to take high-level leadership positions through her Amujae Initiative, which means 'we are going up' in local Liberian dialect. Together with two other former female presidents – Malawi's Joyce Banda (b. 1950) and the Central African Republic's Catherine Samba-Panza (b. 1954) – Sirleaf's initiative is providing mentorship to rising women leaders.

Ellen Johnson Sirleaf, President of Liberia for much of the early 21st century.

THE IMPACT OF OPRAH

Oprah Winfrey (b. 1954) is an American talk show host, actress, television producer and philanthropist. Besides being television's highest-paid entertainer and the first African American woman to own her own production company, she is also a powerful advocate for women's leadership. Winfrey herself was born into poverty in the Jim Crow segregation south of the USA. She has funded initiatives like the Oprah Winfrey Leadership Academy for Girls in South Africa to help young women overcome childhood poverty and trauma and take on leadership roles. Through Oprah's Angel Network and other charitable initiatives, Oprah concentrates much of her philanthropic work on educational grants and leadership mentoring programmes such as Women for Women International and Girl Effect.

Behave 'like a man'?

In some societies, female leadership has been perceived as violating long-established gender norms. As a result, having women in positions of authority can threaten male privilege and power, and provokes resistance. Female leaders challenge sexist stereotypes in patriarchal societies, subverting machismo identities of androcentric institutions. However, in some cases, there is pressure on women to 'behave like a man' to succeed. This includes adopting stereotypical characteristics associated with men in Western societies, such as dominance, bullish confidence and little emotion or empathy. These gender-based stereotypes about political leaders have important implications. Women are less likely to be considered in leadership roles, which impacts on the likelihood that they enter politics. When young girls are socialized into thinking that women are less suited as leaders, they might not see politics as a career option.

Even today, women politicians are subject to immense scrutiny by media and political pundits. They are judged on their appearance in ways that men are not. They are often pressured to perform masculine stereotypes associated with leadership to obtain acceptance but then are represented as aggressive and cold, which can drive voters away. On the other hand, if women do not promote masculinity, they are represented as 'too feminine' to be effective leaders. This places female political leaders in a catch-22 situation as to how they should act.

Women belong in the all the places where decisions are being made.
– Ruth Bader Ginsburg

Androcentrism – the practice of centring one's world view, history and culture around a masculine point of view.

The assertiveness double-bind – There is a double standard for working women and female leaders regarding assertiveness. Women often receive negative personality criticism (as bossy, aggressive or abrasive) whereas the same characteristics are perceived positively in men.

Hillary Clinton, former US First Lady and Secretary of State, speaking during a bruising presidential campaign against Donald Trump in 2016.

Playing the 'woman card'?

Although women are increasingly being elected to political office in greater numbers, female politicians still face major challenges. Research has found that voters project Western feminine stereotypes (such as compassion) onto female candidates while masculine characteristics (such as strength) are expected to apply to male candidates.

Women are making huge strides as leaders in positions of power around the world. Imagine a world where people do not focus on what a female political leader is wearing, but instead on their transformative actions.

The presidential battle between Hillary Clinton and Donald Trump in the USA in 2016 brought increased attention to the treatment of female politicians. Trump questioned Clinton's 'strength' and 'stamina', remarked that she did not have a 'presidential look' and mocked her for 'shouting'. Clinton was routinely name-called (as bossy, abrasive, nasty, shrill, emotional and bitchy) in ways that are common with confident, strong and assertive women who do not conform to traditional female stereotypes. But despite the persistence of aggressive criticism driven by gender bias, Clinton and other female leaders have pushed boundaries and brought conversations about gender bias into the open. Clinton countered Trump's accusation that she was playing the 'woman card', responding, 'if fighting for women's health care, and paid family leave and equal pay is playing the woman card, then deal me in!'

OPPOSITE: *'The Squad' is a group of six left-wing Democratic members of the US House of Representatives. The Squad was initially made up of four congresswomen elected in 2019: Ilhan Omar of Minnesota, Alexandria Ocasio-Cortez of New York, Rashida Tlaib of Michigan and Ayanna Pressley of Massachusetts. All are women of colour and all were elected under the age of 50. After the 2020 US House of Representatives elections, the group expanded to include Jamaal Bowman of New York and Cori Bush of Missouri. They are well known as particularly progressive and heralded as the 'future of the Democratic Party' in representing a younger political generation. They have advanced policies such as a national healthcare system (Medicare for All) and the Green New Deal proposal to address climate change through the creation of green jobs.*

RIGHT: *Brené Brown (b. 1965) is an American social science researcher, writer and lecturer. She is well known for her work on leadership. Her 2010 TEDx talk, 'The Power of Vulnerability', is one of the most viewed TED talks in the world. She advocates for four pillars of courageous leadership: vulnerability, clarity of values, trust and rising skills. In Western society, vulnerability is often seen as a weakness, but she posits that it is, in fact, crucial to strong leadership. Through programmes like COURAGEworks, Brown helps leaders recognize the importance of openness and empathizing, rather than 'armouring up'.* 'I define a leader as anyone who takes responsibility for finding the potential in people and processes, and who has the courage to develop that potential.' – *Brené Brown*

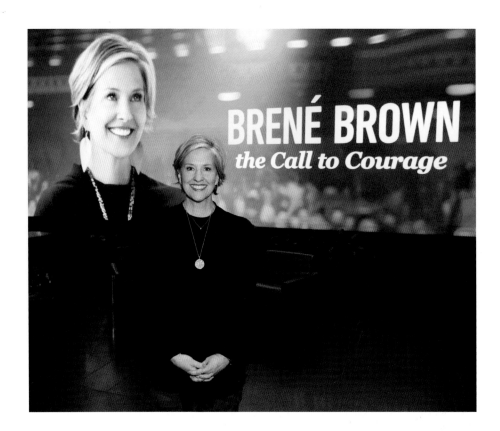

The hidden figures of STEM

One field of work where women have played an important role but have a history of being rendered invisible is in science, technology, engineering and mathematics, better known as STEM. Even though women – and women of colour in particular – are often not recognized in historical records, numerous accounts detail the pivotal role of women in developing new technologies, medical knowledge, engineering skills and scientific instruments.

An early example is the Babylonian chemist Tapputi-Belatekallim (*c.*1200BCE) – a royal perfume maker in ancient Babylon (present-day Iraq). At this time, perfumes were far more than fragrances for beautification: they were required for medicinal purposes. Clay cuneiform texts from the era detail the specialist chemical apparatuses that Tapputi used, including the oldest reference to the distillation apparatus 'the still', versions of which are in use in laboratories to this day.

It was not only Ancient Egypt that had skilled female physicians: the presence of women in medicine, as practising surgeons and physicians, has been traced back to earliest human history. Women held sacred tribal roles in healing, and were engaged in midwifery and healing arts, often with their activities unrecorded. This is due in part to the fact that during the late Middle Ages in Europe, religious doctrines made it very difficult for women healers to practise. Some were mistrusted, labelled as witches, and killed. Several historians have argued that the witch-hunts were a concerted effort to push women out of healthcare. Others have pointed to the professionalization of medicine as the real moment of exclusion of women from the field.

As far back as 2300BCE, Enheduanna, the High Priestess of the goddess Inanna and moon god Nanna in the Sumerian city-state of Ur, studied astronomy and tracked the moon's cycles. She recorded her findings as poetry, like other scientists of her time.

As scientific professions were institutionalized in Europe during the Renaissance period of the 16th and 17th centuries, women's roles were limited in formal medical professions. Unable to access university medical education, they could not obtain medical licences, and the healing profession became completely male dominated. Women were, however, able to formally practise in Europe through 'family businesses' or the guilds. However, it was not until the women's movements of the 1800s that they could practise medicine in a formal and high-profile way.

TRADITIONAL HEALERS

Machis are traditional healers and religious leaders among the Mapuche of Chile and Argentina who have detailed knowledge of medicinal herbs and healing remedies. Women are more commonly *machis* than men, although within *machi* rituals, gender is fluid and new gender identities are explored in order to heal. Mapuche traditional medicine is steadily gaining more acceptance in Chilean society, although *machis* still battle discrimination.

'CUNNING FOLK'

These were folk healers across Europe, many of whom were women, who had in-depth knowledge of herbal remedies. Despite some suggestions that they were persecuted during the period of witch trials, many folk healers actually commanded a great deal of respect and were allowed to practise because of their popularity in their communities. Names given to folk healers in Europe include the French *devins-guérisseurs* (soothsayer-healers), the Irish *bean feasa* (woman of knowledge) and the Finnish *tietäjät* (knowers).

Gertrud Olofsdotter Ahlgren (1782–1874) was a well-known Swedish 'cunning woman' on the island of Gotland. She was very popular for her herbal medicine and is known for once saying, 'the doctors cure by new [methods], illnesses are old and I cure by old [methods].'

An association of pioneering women physicians founded the London School of Medicine for Women in 1874. For many years, it was the only place where a woman could obtain a medical degree in the UK.

THE GLASS CEILING

The 'glass ceiling' is a metaphor that is used to represent the invisible barrier experienced by women and minorities that prevents them from advancing within a hierarchy. Feminists first started using the term in the 1970s to describe the obstacles experienced by women in the workplace. Female physicians faced many forms of discrimination in Europe due to developing attitudes that the ideal woman should act submissively and take a domestic role. Consequently, medical degrees were very difficult for women to obtain and medicine was a major professional battleground where women had to push back against these notions of a woman's 'proper place'. In response, 19th-century pioneers such as English physician Sophia Jex-Blake (1840–1912) established women's medical colleges and hospitals to help women access the profession.

Susan La Flesche

Susan La Flesche (1865–1915) was born on the Omaha Reservation in north-eastern Nebraska and was the first Native American woman in the USA to receive a medical degree. She was an active social reformer as well as a renowned physician. As a child, she witnessed a sick indigenous woman die after a local white doctor refused to give her medical care. This tragedy inspired La Flesche to train as a physician and support those with whom she lived on the reservation.

Women were often healers in Omaha society, but it was rare for any woman in the Victorian era in the USA to go to institutional medical schools, let alone indigenous women or women of colour. But through her perseverance and by galvanizing support networks, La Flesche was able to enter the Woman's Medical College of Pennsylvania – one of the few schools that accepted women. She graduated at the top of her class before returning to the Omaha Reservation in 1889 as a physician. Throughout her career, La Flesche campaigned for public health reforms and for the legal redistribution of land to the Omaha. Even then, as a woman, she could not vote, nor as a Native American could she legally call herself an American citizen.

Susan La Flesche as a young woman.

Top left: Katherine Johnson;
Top right: Christine Darden;
Below left: Dorothy Vaughan;
Below right: Mary Jackson.
The mathematical and scientific
prowess of these four helped
launch the space programme.

NASA's 'Hidden Figures'

Thanks to the book by Margot Lee Shetterly, *Hidden Figures* (2016), and the film of the same name, Katherine Johnson, Dorothy Vaughan, Christine Darden and Mary Jackson have finally been given global recognition. As African American mathematicians and rocket scientists, they worked against enormous racial and gender barriers in the USA to help send mankind into space, providing essential calculations for the orbital trajectories of rockets. Following an overwhelming response to the film, 21st Century Fox and the US Department of State launched the #HiddenNoMore initiative. The programme brings emerging female leaders in STEM from around the world to the USA to enhance opportunities for women in STEM in their own countries.

The Nobel Prize winners behind the scenes

Women have been overwhelmingly underrepresented as Nobel Prize winners in the sciences since the awards began in 1901. Named after the Swedish chemist Alfred Nobel, the Nobel Prizes are awarded in physics, chemistry, physiology or medicine, economic sciences, literature and peace. From the start, Nobel recipients have disproportionately been white men from Western countries. Of all 972 Nobel recipients from 1901 to 2021, only 58 have been women. Women account for only 3 per cent of science-category winners and have been almost always been awarded the prize jointly with male colleagues. Yet, despite not receiving the recognition, women have been at the helm of many scientific discoveries that achieved Nobel Prizes, with the award going to their male colleagues.

Chien-Shiung Wu

Chien-Shiung Wu (1912–97) was a Chinese American physicist who conducted experiments with radioactive cobalt to make extraordinary contributions to the field. But despite Wu's work, it was her male colleagues who won the 1957 Nobel Prize in Physics.

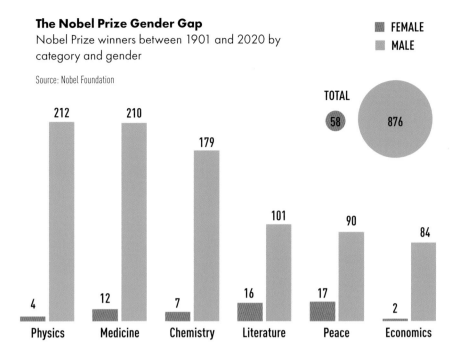

The Nobel Prize Gender Gap
Nobel Prize winners between 1901 and 2020 by category and gender

Source: Nobel Foundation

- FEMALE
- MALE

TOTAL
58 / 876

Category	Female	Male
Physics	4	212
Medicine	12	210
Chemistry	7	179
Literature	16	101
Peace	17	90
Economics	2	84

The Nobel Prize awarding body has come under fire in recent years for still concentrating recognition on white Western men. Many female scientists have made outstanding contributions, but never became laureates. Instead, it has been their male colleagues who have taken the credit.

Chien-Shiung Wu pictured at work.

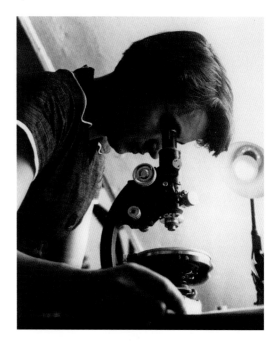

Esther Lederberg

This was also the case with Esther Lederberg (1922–2006), the microbiologist and pioneer of bacterial genetics. Her contributions to microbiology were enormous, including the discovery of lambda phage (key in the study of genetics) and techniques that allow scientists to replicate bacterial colonies to the establishment of Stanford University's Plasmid Reference Center. However, it was her husband who received the Nobel Prize in 1958, despite the fact that much of the work was performed by Esther herself. She also had to fight for her faculty position at Stanford and never received tenure.

Rosalind Franklin

The chemist Rosalind Franklin's (1920–58) contributions were critical to our understandings of DNA structure. She used an X-ray analysis technique to photograph the distinctive double-helical structure of DNA. Her photographs were published by her male colleagues and she was not given credit. They received the Nobel Prize in 1962 for her work, with Franklin completely disregarded, after her death from ovarian cancer.

Marie Curie

Marie Curie (1867–1934) was the first woman to receive a Nobel Prize in Physics, in 1903 with her husband for the discovery of radioactivity. Then, in 1911, she was the sole winner of the Nobel Prize in Chemistry for her work on isolating pure radium.

Marie Curie in her laboratory in Paris.

THE 'MATILDA EFFECT'

This term was coined by science historian Margaret Rossiter (b. 1944) and named after the suffragist Matilda Joslyn Gage (1826–98), who first described the effect. It details the bias women scientists often experience, whereby their work and achievements are attributed to their male colleagues. One of the earliest recorded incidents of this is Trota, an Italian physician from the 12th century. She gained fame across Europe for her radical study of female anatomy and medical treatments, but her works – compiled in the *Trotula* treatises – were attributed to her husband and son.

Matilda Effect

Scientific efforts and achievements of women do not receive the same recognition as do those of men.

She didn't do it.
She did it, but she shouldn't have.
She did it, but look what she did.
She did it, but she did only part of it.
She did it, but she had help.
She did it, BUT ...

@DrawInScience @IlustraConCiencia

WOMEN IN SPACE

Women have contributed enormously to space exploration since the earliest days, as scientists and astronauts: China, Russia, Iran, India, Japan and the USA all have major space programmes in which women actively take part.

Valentina Tereshkova
In 1963, the Soviet cosmonaut Valentina Tereshkova (b. 1937) made history as the first and youngest woman in space. She is still the only woman to have flown a solo space mission.

Sally Ride

The physicist Sally Ride (1951–2012) was the first American woman to fly in space. Ride's historic flight, in 1983 – and that of the two Soviet astronauts before her – became symbolic of the ability of women to shatter glass ceilings and reach for the stars.

Mae Jemison

Mae Jemison (b. 1956) became the first Black woman to travel into space. She is a doctor, engineer and NASA astronaut who has gone on to found her own company, the Jemison Group, which focuses on encouraging a love of science among schoolchildren.

The Emirati mechanical engineer Nora Al Matrooshi (b. 1993) has been selected as the first Arab woman to train as an astronaut. She would be the 66th woman to travel into space.

The future of women in space

As space travel becomes more commonplace, through private programmes such as SpaceX and Blue Origin, more female astronauts will likely follow in the trailblazing footsteps of Tereshkova, Ride, Jemison and others. Organizations like 'Rocket Women' are empowering young women to focus on a career in STEM as astronauts, scientists and engineers.

The Woman's Suffrage Procession was a carefully choreographed event that attracted thousands of women and some arresting pageantry. It was held the day before the inauguration of US president Woodrow Wilson, in an attempt to highlight the iniquity of women being unable to exercise their democratic rights.

4 WOMEN AND SOCIAL CHANGE

Women have been and continue to be crucial to social justice movements around the world. They have led the charge in mobilizing collective action strategies to combat all forms of inequality, including sexual exploitation, restrictions on their ability to own property, the right to vote, geographical disadvantages and access to healthcare.

Women's movements across time and place

In September 2021, more than 5,000 indigenous women marched through Brazil's capital to protest at Bolsonaro's government's attempts to roll back indigenous land rights and open up their territories to extractive mining operations and agribusiness. These efforts form part of a centuries-long attempt to erase the indigenous descendants of Brazil's first inhabitants prior to Portuguese colonization in 1500. In recent decades, indigenous women have become visible leaders at the forefront of environmental movements in Brazil and around the world.

A woman from the Pataxo tribe during a demonstration for the demarcation of indigenous land in Brasilia, on 8 September 2021.

In the Brazilian Caruna Indigenous Territory, for example, where some of the last intact Amazonian rainforest exists, Guajajira women are taking roles as 'Guerreiras da Floresta' ('women warriors of the forest'). The *guerreiras* embark on lengthy forest patrols to monitor and protect the forests from logging and land invasions. By building social ties and focusing on educating neighbouring communities about the forests, the *guerreiras* are advocating for a public attitudinal shift towards stewardship over exploitation. Through their efforts, they have dramatically reduced deforestation in the region and publicly defined their roles as female leaders and protectors.

Like the *guerreiras*, women have long come together within and across countries to effect change in the face of injustices. These many organizing efforts often share common concerns of labour equality,

economic independence, family, childbirth, childcare and improving women's positions in society. However, they also hold important political, economic and cultural differences. Examining different forms of protest reveals how women utilize the power of collective gender identities for social subversiveness or self-empowerment and to mobilize against dominant hierarchies. Making cross-cultural comparisons also shows that there is no 'correct' universal feminism.

Western women's suffrage – the right to vote in political elections – is often distinguished as the first transnational women's movement. However, this Eurocentric perspective surrounding women's activism marginalizes diverse feminist organizing efforts around the world. The suffrage movement was crucial for securing the right of women to vote in many countries, but focusing on the suffrage work of white female elites creates a limited picture. While there might not be written evidence of social movements among different societies, that does not mean they did not exist. This emphasis on white Western feminism overlooks the reality that some women of colour in non-Western societies already had voting rights and lived within alternative gender hierarchies. In fact, it was the political egalitarianism of Haudenosaunee (Iroquois) women that inspired early American suffragettes.

Feminism, as a belief in the equality of women, is rooted in the earliest ages of human civilization. The Hindu Bhakti movement originated in southern India in the seventh century. The movement pivoted on religious egalitarianism with the view that everyone is equal in the eyes of God. These religious principles became important precursors to early feminist movements in India. Many women and those from low-caste backgrounds joined regional Bhakti movements to move out of domestic spaces and protest against oppressive hierarchies and the rigidity of India's caste-based system.

> **Feminism** – a belief in the political, economic and cultural equality of women. Feminism can take many forms. Some people reject the term 'feminist' because it aligns too closely with white middle-class Western constructs.

> **Eurocentric** – taking European or Western culture as the centre of the universe and as a measurement against which all other cultures are judged, largely as inferior. The term is used to critique Western narratives of 'developed' versus 'underdeveloped' and the marginalization of non-Western practices and viewpoints.

Women were important poets in the Bhakti movement. Akka Mahadevi was a Bhakti poet from southern India in the 12th century. In her poetry, she voiced her frustrations with societal norms and gender restrictions in India.

Women's rights under colonialism: Indonesia

Women's movements are specific to time and place. It was generally not suffrage that first inspired women's activism in many non-Western regions. Instead, women's struggles connected to the subservience of life under colonial rule.

The colonial social order in what is now Indonesia, but then the Dutch East Indies, was based on made-up racial and social structures. Race was used to categorize people as so-called 'civilized' or 'primitive' and justify colonial rule. At this time, many Indonesian women were employed as servants and nannies to the Dutch white elite.

Colonialism, as the control by one power over another area or people, was a violent project that resulted in dramatic upheavals. From the 1500s, many regions of the world experienced the brutalities of European rule in the quest for gold, silver and other forms of wealth, as well as European dreams of power and the establishment of permanent settlements. The spread of religion also motivated exploration, with colonization and settlement closely linked to a desire to bring Christianity around the world through crusading

LEFT: *A plaque commemorating the Dutch East India Company on a building in Hoorn in the Netherlands.*

BELOW: *Raden Ajeng Kartini (1879–1904) has long been considered the symbol of female empowerment in Indonesia. Born to an aristocratic family in Java, Kartini was unable to access education because of Javanese prohibitions against young girls attending school. She went on to use her family's connections with the Dutch government to lobby for the first Indonesian primary school for Indonesian girls to be opened in 1903.*

expeditions. These explorations often resulted in violent patterns of colonization, with little concern for the livelihoods of indigenous inhabitants beyond the exploitation of their natural resources.

Women in particular experienced extreme brutalities under colonialism, for instance when the Dutch colonized the Indonesian islands – one of their most valuable colonies for its spice and cash-crop trade – across the 18th century. During this time, many Indonesian women were pushed into becoming the servants and sexual partners of Dutch white men.

Feminism and movements for women's rights in Indonesia began under Dutch rule in retaliation to this treatment. These were based upon pushing for educational opportunities for women, as well as campaigns around providing sex education. These goals provided women with alternative avenues. Through education, they could move outside of traditional Indonesian domestic norms and the subservience of Dutch colonial rule.

During this period, women's rights organizations and movements developed under Budi Utomo, the first Indonesian nationalist organization. Nationalistic aspirations for independence from colonial rule intersected with issues such as education and women's rights in marriage. For most of the first half of the 20th century through to Indonesia's independence in 1945, the Indonesian women's movement was a part of the nationalist movement against Dutch colonial rule. This focus provided added momentum to Indonesia's independence from colonialism, but it also limited the emphasis on women's struggles against patriarchal norms.

'NINE KARTINIS OF KENDENG'

Women in Indonesia still draw on Kartini's ideologies to put forward their social justice goals. The 'Nine Kartinis of Kendeng' is a group of female farmers who have been fighting against the construction of a cement factory in Rembang in central Java. They say that the factory would be environmentally devastating and would dry up the local springs on which their agricultural practices and economic livelihoods depend. By staging powerful protests with their feet buried in cement blocks in front of the presidential palace in Jakarta in 2016, the women became iconic images of farmers' resistance in Indonesia.

Putri Mardika (1912) was the first women's organization in Indonesia. It focused on gender objectives and independence for Indonesia.

Women's rights under colonialism: the Igbo Women's War (*Ogu Umunwanyi*)

Prior to colonialism, Nigeria was a series of powerful city-states. The region is home to more than 250 ethnic groups speaking 500 different languages. Nigeria was colonially governed by the British Empire from the region's annexation in 1861 until independence in 1960. Colonial rule dramatically changed the position of Nigerian women. Previously, they had a prominent political presence. In some regions, such as Igboland in south-eastern Nigeria, women participated in local governance and held major economic roles in the marketplace. They were respected members of society, took part in village meetings and had strong solidarity groups. However, British colonial authorities tried to assert control by pushing against these traditional power distributions. For example, they attempted to impose a patriarchal Victorian system on very different gender arrangements. This included elevating political institutions led by Igbo men and ignoring those of women.

A 60th Aniversary re-enactment of the Women's Protest during the Igbo Women's War.

Disenfranchisement from political economic life was coupled with greater taxation, leading many women in Nigeria to become increasingly frustrated with colonial rule. They responded in a variety of ways to the patriarchal situation they found themselves in, from subtle through to more overt, and at times violent, forms of resistance.

The Igbo Women's War was a series of protests that broke out in November 1929. It is often seen as the first major challenge to British colonial rule. In order to control Nigeria through forms of 'indirect' rule, the British had organized Igboland into Native Court areas. These regions were governed by a local warrant chief chosen by the British administration. Under this new colonial system, Igbo people were at the mercy of the warrant chiefs. Women in particular suffered because warrant chiefs

NIGERIAN WOMEN AND COLLECTIVE ACTION

Nigeria has a long history of female collective action. Women often organized strikes and boycotts through their kinship and market networks to push for social change. In 1910, women in Agbaja withdrew from local life to protest at an increase in female mortality. They left their husbands' villages and went with their mats to sleep in the local marketplaces until their demands were met. In the 1940s, the Abeokuta Women's Union led a resistance movement to oppose unfair taxation by the Nigerian colonial

government. Female labour unions such as the Lagos Market Women Association have been important ways for women to organize collective action and defend their ability to earn a living for themselves and their families.

confiscated their livestock, profited from their market sales and restricted the role of women in government. Colonial administrators heightened these local grievances when they announced the imposition of special taxes on Igbo market women.

Because women no longer had political power, thanks to the patriarchal system of colonial rule, they used collective action to put forward their dissatisfaction. Thousands of Igbo women from eastern Nigeria mobilized in the town of Oloko. They led sit-ins and ransacked a number of Native Courts set up by the British, forcing many warrant chiefs to resign. The two months of protest were on a scale never seen before in the British colonial state, with at least 25,000 women involved. Fifty-five women were killed in the protests by colonial troops and many more were wounded.

Madame Nwanyeruwa played a key role in the Women's War. She advocated for non-violent protest strategies, including traditional all-night song-and-dance rituals (known as 'sitting on a man', see box) to force the warrant chiefs to resign. She inspired women in other villages to advance their own political movements against colonial and patriarchal rule.

'SITTING ON A MAN'

'Sitting on a man' is a traditional strategy of conflict resolution used by Igbo women. It involves publicly shaming a man by dancing, singing, detailing his behaviour or beating the walls or roof of his home. This method of resistance functioned as a way for women to maintain the balance of social and political power during the pre-colonial era. In the British colonial context, the political force of the practice came from its powerful affront to Victorian mores of female subservience.

Ultimately, the women achieved their aims. In 1930, the British colonial government abolished the warrant chieftain system, and appointed women in the Native Courts. As a result, women's movements grew stronger and more united across the colonial state. These reforms were steadily built on by West African women, leading to the emergence of collective African nationalism and pushes for independence.

Female-led movements continue to demand visibility for those made invisible in Nigeria. In 2014, the #BringBackOurGirls movement brought global awareness to the 276 schoolgirls kidnapped by the extremist Islamic group Boko Haram. The largely Christian female students were kidnapped by Boko Haram from their secondary school in Chibok in Nigeria on the night of 14 April 2014. Some of the girls escaped, but over 100 are still missing. Boko Haram continues to use the girls as negotiating pawns in exchange for the release of their captured members in jail, as well as a way to gain media visibility. The Chibok schoolgirls' kidnapping is only a small percentage of those abducted by Boko Haram.

Former Nigerian Education Minister and Vice-President of the World Bank's Africa division (3rd L) Obiageli Ezekwesilieze speaks as she leads a march of Nigerian women and mothers of the kidnapped girls of Chibok, calling for their freedom in Abuja on 30 April 2014.

The Western suffrage movement

The Western suffrage movement was the culmination of centuries of discontent and resistance by women and their male allies. The first wave of the movement began in the mid-19th century in Europe and North America. Suffragism – the right to vote – was central to women's struggles at the time. However, women were also pushing for female emancipation more broadly. This included access to employment and education, and the abolition of 'coverture', which made women the legal property of their husbands. The system of coverture had developed in England in the Middle Ages, whence it spread to many common law jurisdictions across the British Empire and settler colonial regions such as North America.

Leading suffragettes Annie Kenney and Cristabel Pankhurst.

These demands were radical at the time. They pushed against the Western ideology of womanhood enshrined in the four tenets of purity, piety, submission and domesticity. According to this viewpoint, white women were located naturally in the household. They were unfit for public, political participation or earning a waged labour in the economic system. However, being largely defined and lead by white middle-class women, such movement priorities excluded the concerns of working-class women and women of colour, who had to work outside of the home, often by necessity. Moreover, Black women had been systematically denied access to the category of 'woman'. Many working women knew that the right to vote in itself would not upend race and class inequalities.

Men make the moral code and they expect women to accept it. They have decided that it is entirely right and proper for men to fight for their liberties and their rights, but that it is not right and proper for women to fight for theirs.
– Emmeline Pankhurst, *My Own Story* (1914).

A GLOBAL MOVEMENT

Most women's rights organizations were connected to suffrage movements in other countries, making female suffrage the first occasion for international mobilization around women's rights.

Vast crowds watch the funeral procession of English suffragette Emily Davison who died after being trampled by the King's horse at the Derby.

African American feminists such as Sojourner Truth (c.1797–1883) pushed for racial justice and women's rights as interlinked goals. After years of brutal enslavement, Truth became a religious speaker and then a powerful opponent to racial and gender inferiority and inequality. Her speech, 'Ain't I A Woman', at the 1851 Women's Rights Convention in Ohio was a powerful call for equal human rights for all women, not just white women.

FEME COVERTS

In English law, as a feme covert (or *femme couverte*), a married woman could not own property, obtain an education without her husband's permission, retain a salary, sign legal documents or enter into contractual arrangements.

Early foundations

The Western women's rights movement was building on foundations of centuries of feminist thought, including that of Christine de Pizan (1364–c.1430) in the 15th century, Modesta di Pozzo di Forzi (1555–92) in the 16th century and Marie de Gournay (1565–1645) in the 17th century. Two of the most important figures who inspired the feminist movements of the 18th and 19th centuries were Mary Wollstonecraft and Olympe de Gouges. Both brought attention to feminist concerns that heavily influenced the aims of women's rights movements, including the #MeToo or the fourth-wave feminist movement that we are familiar with today.

A portrait of Mary Wollstonecraft painted by John Opie c.1797.

Olympe de Gouges as painted by Alexander Kucharsky in the late 18th century.

Mary Wollstonecraft

Mary Wollstonecraft (1759–97) was a seminal British feminist thinker and writer, and one of the most important influences on the Western suffrage movement. Her A *Vindication of the Rights of Woman* (1792) challenged political figures at the time who advocated against women having an education beyond the domestic. In it, she argued that women are not naturally inferior to men but deserving of the same fundamental rights of all human beings.

Olympe de Gouges

Olympe de Gouges (1748–93) was writing at the same time as Wollstonecraft, also bringing women's rights to the forefront of European political debates. She was a French playwright and political activist who wrote widely on women's rights and the abolition of slavery. Her *Declaration of the Rights of Woman and of the Female Citizen* (1791) was a powerful response to the French Assembly's *Declaration of the Rights of the Man and of the Citizen* (1789), in which she voiced female oppression. As a result of her writings, de Gouges was convicted of treason and beheaded. She is now publicly honoured in street and building names across France.

The four waves of feminism

Western women's movements are generally characterized in four waves. However, this wave imagery has been criticized for erasing histories of activism. With this description, one might think feminism's history is a coherent arc led by Euro-American campaigners. In reality, many sub-movements built on – and fought with – one another in the push for gender equality. Nevertheless, this typology is helpful in distinguishing between different progressions of feminist movements and overall shifts in aims.

The first wave of feminism began in the late 19th and early 20th centuries, often marked by the Seneca Falls Convention of 1848: the first women's rights convention in the USA. Three hundred people were part of the convention, where one of the lead organizers, Elizabeth Cady Stanton, famously drafted the Seneca Falls Declaration, outlining the movement's ideology and political strategies. African American abolitionist Frederick Douglass, an early champion of women's

rights, also spoke powerfully in support. First-wave feminists were influenced by the collective activism of women across other reform movements, including the abolitionist movement against slavery and the temperance movement against alcohol. Movement leaders were also inspired by their observations of differing gender roles beyond Euro-American societies.

Haudenosaunee Native American political structure partly inspired the frame of government of the USA created by revolutionary leaders after the American War of Independence in the late 1700s. But, unlike the Haudenosaunee model, women were excluded from decision making and power. To this day, Haudenosaunee women play powerful roles in social movements. This includes taking part in national women's marches, to make visible interconnected concerns surrounding gender, racial and ethnic discrimination.

First wave	1848 to 1950s	Women's suffrage, right to property, political power and equality of treatment.
Second wave	1960s to 1980s	Broadened to critique a wider range of male-dominated institutions and cultural practices, including de facto and official legal inequalities relating to domesticity, family, sexuality, reproductive rights and the workplace.
Third wave	1990s to 2000s	Centred on diversity and individualism, including focused efforts to recognize the layers of oppression caused by gender, race and class. American theorists in the 1980s and '90s, such as the law professor Kimberlé Crenshaw, made this clear in work on the concept of 'intersectionality'. The sociologist Judith Butler's insights into the performativity of gender were foundational to the fight for trans rights as a crucial part of intersectional feminism.
Fourth wave	2008 to present	Utilization of social media platforms to mobilize and collaborate for the empowerment of women and seek justice against harassment and sexual assault, such as the #MeToo movement. It argues for greater political and business representation for women and trans people by extending gender-equal opportunities in workplace policies and emotional expression.

Y^E MAY SESSION OF Y^E WOMAN'S RIGHTS CONVENTION—Y^E ORATOR OF Y^E DAY DENOUNCING Y^E LORDS OF CREATION.

Seneca Falls (1848) was the first women's rights convention held in the USA. It was held in Seneca Falls, New York, an area that is part of the Haudenosaunee (Iroquois) Confederacy territory. This was no accident. The movement's leaders were inspired by Haudenosaunee gender-egalitarian models of organizing society.

INSPIRING FIRST-WAVE FEMINISM: HAUDENOSAUNEE (IROQUOIS) WOMEN AND POLITICS

The American suffrage movement was partially inspired by the involvement of Haudenosaunee women in politics. Unlike European American women in the 19th century, Haudenosaunee women held – and still hold – tremendous political authority. Like a number of First Nations people in North America, the Haudenosaunee have a matrilineal kinship system. Property, child custody and lineage pass through the female line. Women participate in all major areas of decision making, including the power to veto acts of war. Although, at the time, the principal chief of the Haudenosaunee Confederacy was a man, women elders selected the chiefs and could also depose them. Women worked in the fields and managed agricultural resources, while sharing governance of the Confederacy. This political economic reality inspired leaders of the American women's rights movement, such as Matilda Joslyn Gage (1826–98), Lucretia Mott (1793–1880) and Elizabeth Cady Stanton (1815–1902). They wrote and spoke about their experiences with Haudenosaunee leaders as proof that women's disenfranchisement was not natural or inevitable.

Haudenosaunee political structure partly inspired the frame of government of the USA created by revolutionary leaders after the American War of Independence in the late 1700s. But unlike the Haudenosaunee model, women were excluded from decision-making and power. To this day, Haudenosaunee women play powerful roles in social movements. This includes taking part in national women's marches, to make visible interconnected concerns surrounding gender, racial and ethnic discrimination.

LEFT: *The Executive Committee of the National Woman Suffrage Association, which was founded by Elizabeth Cady Stanton and Susan B Anthony in 1869.*

Women's rights and racial justice

Suffragist movements made significant contributions towards women's rights. However, they were also subject to internal disputes and divisions. American feminism holds a toxic history of racism. Black suffragists often experienced discrimination from being a part of national white suffrage movements. Some white suffragists, like Stanton and Anthony, were outspokenly racist in pushing for the right of women to vote over Black men; others courted white Southern women who supported slavery.

Elizabeth Cady Stanton

As a writer, lecturer and principal philosopher of the women's rights movement, Elizabeth Cady Stanton (1815–1902) led the struggle for gender equality in the USA. She formed decades-long partnerships with Susan B. Anthony and Lucretia Mott that were crucial to the movement's development. Stanton was also involved in abolitionism, but her focus on women's rights moved her to adopt racist positions. She prioritized the concerns of middle-class white women instead of creating solidarities across race and class. This resulted in a split with her once close ally, Frederick Douglass, and other women's rights activists such as Frances Watkins Harper. This rift was heightened when Stanton condemned the 15th Amendment, which gave Black men the right to vote, but not women.

Elizabeth Cady Stanton c.1880 when she was 65.

Frances Watkins Harper

Frances Watkins Harper (1825–1911) was an American abolitionist, suffragist, public speaker, educator and writer. She was one of the first African American women to be published in the USA, having a successful literary career. As an activist, Harper advanced an intersectional approach that brought together her work in African American civil rights with advocating for women's rights. She spoke out about the specific discrimination she faced not just as a woman but as a Black woman. Harper pushed for African American suffrage and women's suffrage to be considered together in the campaign for equal rights. This led to a break with other movement leaders like Stanton and Anthony, who were critical about Black men having a vote before white women.

Mary Church Terrell

Mary Church Terrell (1863–1954) was a prominent African American activist for civil rights and suffrage in the USA. She was a teacher in Washington, D.C. at the first African American public high school in the country, going on to become the first African American woman in the USA to be appointed to a major city's school board. She was the leader of the National Association of Colored Women and co-founder of the National Association for the Advancement of Colored People. Throughout her career, she pushed for racial justice and women's rights to be interlinked goals.

Mary Church Terrell in the early 20th century.

A sketch of Frances Watkins Harper.

Ida B Wells-Barnett.

Emmeline Pankhurst.

Ida B. Wells-Barnett

Ida B. Wells-Barnett (1862–1931) was a journalist, activist and researcher who shed light on the brutalities faced by African Americans in the South. She published powerful work exposing the lynching taking place in the southern USA. This led white supremacist mobs to burn down her press in Memphis, Tennessee, eventually forcing her to move to Chicago. She was a founder of the National Association of Colored Women's Clubs, an organization created to address the intersections of civil rights and women's suffrage.

Emmeline Pankhurst

Emmeline Pankhurst (1858–1928) was a British political activist who led the early women's rights movement in the UK. Pankhurst advanced direct-action strategies and a policy of 'deeds, not words'. This included physical demonstrations, window smashing, arson and hunger strikes. One member of Pankhurst's Women's Social and Political Union (WSPU), Emily Davison (1872–1913), tragically threw herself under King George V's horse at the Royal Derby as part of a protest against the continued lack of votes for women.

Just as today's protestors utilize the power of social media, the suffragettes also recognized the power of the press. Emmeline Pankhurst, together with her daughters Sylvia, Christabel and Adela, led the WPSU to conduct a nationwide arson and bombing campaign across the UK. The WPSU burned down MPs' homes, churches and post offices, bombed train stations and smashed windows in London's Oxford Street. Those arrested would go on high-profile hunger strikes. The WPSU's protest techniques led to direct conflicts with other female activists at the time, who disagreed with strategies of militant violence.

Following years of struggle, women achieved the right to vote. New Zealand was the first self-governing country where all women had the right to vote, from 1893. This was soon followed by other countries, including Finland in 1906: the first European country to do so. The majority of Western powers legalized women's voting during the interwar period, including Canada in 1917, the UK, Poland and Germany in 1918, Austria and the Netherlands in 1919, and the USA in 1920 in the 19th Amendment. It was no coincidence that these reforms came at this time. Women's participation in World War I (1914–18) had challenged false beliefs of women's physical and intellectual inferiority.

THE 'SUFF-BIRDS' AND STRATEGIES OF PROTEST

With the dawn of the 20th century, and their demands still unmet, determined women adopted creative and dramatic tactics of protest to push for women's right to vote. They organized parades, pageants and 'suffrage trains', and even threw Votes for Women leaflets out of biplanes and hot air balloons. Pioneering female aviators who supported these missions (known as 'suff-birds') included the American pilot Leda Richberg-Hornsby (1886–1939). She was the first female graduate of the Wright Flying School. As a woman, she had been refused entry into the US flying corps as a combat pilot.

Some suffragettes – notably in the UK – were more radical in their methods of pursuing suffrage. They used forms of civil disobedience, engaging in what Pankhurst called a women's 'civil war'.

In many countries, women were heavily involved in World War I. As 'canary girls' (so called because their work stained them yellow), British women worked in munitions factories, manufacturing trinitrotoluene (TNT) shells. This sort of participation challenged erroneous beliefs about women's strength that blocked them from voting.

Accessing the vote in colonial contexts

In some regions and societies around the world, women already had political voting rights. Colonialism resulted in major setbacks for women's rights. The 19th Amendment initially excluded women of the USA's incorporated territories from the right to vote. Queen Lili'uokalani (1838–1917) was the last sovereign of the Hawaiian kingdom. Before Hawaii's annexation by the USA in 1898, women held significant roles in government. It was not until decades later that women in Hawaii, along with other American colonies, regained the right to vote, and still more before they could hold political power in determining their region's future.

Since Saudi Arabia gave voting rights to women in 2015, women can vote in all countries that have general elections.

Queen Lili'uokalani of Hawaii c.1891.

The reproductive justice debate

Birth control or contraception has a long history around the world in providing women with the ability to control their reproductive capacity. Among many cultures past and present, abortion – a procedure to end a pregnancy either by taking medicines or through surgery – has had varying stigmas. In many places, abortion is an accepted measure to prevent pregnancy. In other instances, such forms of family planning are criticized for social and religious reasons. Yet, in cases where abortion is inaccessible or even rendered illegal, unsafe abortions, performed using dangerous methods, are a leading – but highly preventable – cause of maternal death and morbidities. Globally, unsafe abortions account for 4.7–13.2 per cent of maternal deaths, disproportionately affecting poor people, people of colour and people in developing regions.

Abortion was not criminalized throughout much of Western history. Some religious orders, such as the Catholic Church, deemed efforts to prevent pregnancy immoral. But despite these regulations, women used a number of different measures to prevent pregnancy, including herbs to control fertility and, at times, infanticide after birth.

Condoms also have a long-documented history, used to reduce the probability of pregnancy or sexually transmitted infections. Condoms were first documented in Europe in 1564 by the Italian anatomist and physician, Gabriele Falloppio (1523–62), who gave his name to the Fallopian tube in the human female reproductive system. In Japan and China, male condoms were used before the 15th century. Condoms in Japan were made of tortoiseshell and then later thin leather. In China, as in 18th-century Europe, condoms were made of oiled paper or animal intestine. One of the first reusable female condoms, made of vulcanized rubber with a coil rim, became popular in Europe in the 1900s.

In some countries, access to reproductive controls have become heated battlegrounds, most notably in the

Abortion has a long medical history. Many civilizations across history also debated the rights of a woman's control over her pregnancy. However, women throughout history did not always have access to safe procedures. In this 13th-century depiction, a herbalist prepares a pennyroyal flower oil abortifacient (or abortion-inducing medicine), which was highly toxic and linked to liver injury and death.

Birth control and abortions were accepted and well documented in ancient Egypt, Greece and Rome. The Ebers Papyrus and the Kahun Papyri from Egypt detail some of the earliest description of birth control, including the use of acacia gum, which is still an ingredient in contraceptive jelly, as well as crocodile dung! Although crocodile dung has spermicidal properties, it is likely a more effective contraceptive than an abortifacient.

ROE V. WADE (1973)

This was a landmark decision of the US Supreme Court. The Court ruled that the US Constitution gave people the right to legally access abortion across the country. The decision struck down a number of state and federal abortion laws and fuelled an ongoing debate about the legality of abortion.

USA. Before 1840, abortion was an often stigma-free, accessible experience for women there. A variety of healers focused on women's reproductive healthcare competed with physicians for business. In order to corner and regulate the market, physicians sought governmental licensing and anti-abortion laws to undermine their opponents. By 1900, every state had laws explicitly forbidding abortion, but with the exception that licensed physicians could carry out abortions to preserve the mother's life. These laws made doctors the gatekeepers of the legality and morality of abortions and created a vast black market for women unable to access abortions through legal medical channels. In the 1960s, the growing feminist movement argued that it was only by controlling reproduction that women could be fully autonomous citizens. They pushed state legislatures to overhaul their abortion laws, including Colorado in 1967, California in 1967 and New York in 1970. These abortion reform efforts gave rise to the anti-abortion or pro-life movement, comprised largely of Catholic doctors, nurses and housewives and supported by the National Council of Catholic Bishops.

Since Roe v. Wade, the USA has remained a battleground for pro-choice and pro-life debates. Those against abortion argue that abortion is an act of killing that terminates a human life. Some critics assert that abortion damages women's bodies and results in post-traumatic stress. On the other hand, those in favour of choice argue that women should have control over their bodies and their lives. In the pro-choice view, legalizing abortion prevents deaths from unsafe, illegal abortions and increases the likelihood that children are born wanted. Many argue that women with financial means simply travel to less restrictive countries for abortions. As a result, closing clinics and criminalizing abortion overwhelmingly affects poor women and women of colour in rural areas and right-wing states.

LEFT: *A pro-choice activist (centre) pictured amongst pro-life activists as they demonstrate in front of the US Supreme Court during the March For Life in Washington, DC on 27 January 2017.*

BELOW: *The USA is in the minority when it comes to reproductive rights policies. Many countries have a number of accredited safe abortion providers and fully cover or subsidize the costs of abortion. In 2018, a referendum in Ireland paved the way for abortion until 12 weeks or longer in the case of preventing serious health issues or death for the mother or foetus.*

Reproductive justice, not pro-choice

Reproductive justice is a concept that was coined in 1994 by a group of African American women in recognition that the predominantly white middle-class pro-choice movement does not fully address poor and low-income women, and especially women of colour. They argued that the rhetoric of 'choice' privileges majority white middle-class women, who

have the possibility of choosing from reproductive options unavailable to many women. Marginalized women have challenges accessing abortion even in regions where it is legal. The creators of reproductive justice argued that the pro-choice framework hides how marginalized women often do not have self-determination over their reproductive lives.

Reproductive justice advocates also critiqued how the mainstream reproductive rights movement focuses almost entirely on the legal right to abortion. However, in the USA, family planning holds racist and eugenicist histories from the left and right of politics. In the early 20th century, family planning activists campaigned for the reproductive control of 'unfit' populations. Indigenous, Latin, Black and disabled women were subject to forced sterilization because of the devaluation of their right to give birth and have children.

Recognizing these problematic histories, reproductive justice examines reproductive health and rights through a social justice and human rights framework to fight for:

- The right to have a child.
- The right not to have a child.
- The right to parent the children we have in safe and healthy conditions regardless of age, race, gender, sexual orientation, immigration status, ability or economic condition.
- The right to bodily autonomy.

In 2004, activists pushed for the March for Choice to become the March for Women's Lives. With more than 1.3 million participants, it was one of the largest protests in US history at the time.

Team SisterSong

SisterSong is the USA's largest organization centred on reproductive justice for women of colour. Headquartered in Atlanta, Georgia, the collective focuses on the southern USA in order to meet the needs of the most marginalized people of colour, including young mothers, those with low incomes, disabilities, criminal backgrounds, HIV/AIDS, sex workers and LGBTQ+ people. They address pressing issues in the reproductive lives of women of colour, including challenges accessing birth control options, unsafe drinking water, food security, police brutality and the separation of parents from children as a result of biased incarceration practices.

Team SisterSong as pictured on their website.

First Nations women against gendered violence

First Nations women have fronted protests across Australia in recent years to spotlight the continued violence experienced by indigenous women since settler colonization. Violence against indigenous women is deeply embedded in Australia's colonial history. Prior to British settlement in 1778, more than 500 First Nations groups inhabited what is now called Australia: custodians of the world's oldest continuous living culture. From 1770, when Captain James Cook first claimed possession of eastern Australia for the British Crown, the First Nations population living on the continent was subject to violence and assault. In the 10 years following the establishment of a penal colony in the newly claimed territory, the indigenous population was reduced by 90 per cent.

From the start, First Nations Aboriginal women, in particular, fought against gendered violence perpetrated by white colonists. Women and girls were regularly sexually assaulted and murdered by colonists. Children were forcibly removed from their parents as part of colonial assimilationist policies that were only later recognized as a form of genocide. In religious missions and so-called native boarding schools, designed to 'civilize' and 'foster habits of decency', children were subject to widespread sexual abuse. Once self-sufficient nomadic peoples were forced into reserves that dispossessed them of their mobility and independence and made them reliant on European food and welfare for survival. Ongoing economic exclusion and cultural decimation led alcoholism and drug addiction to ravage indigenous communities. Women had to contend not only with the cultural destruction of their lifeways, but also with the violence of racism and sexism. The British colonial administration relegated First Nations women to second-class status, rendering them invisible.

The Great Australian Silence

The sexual violence perpetrated by white settlers against Aboriginal women remains relatively unspoken of to this day, part of a long-term trend known as 'the Great Australian Silence'. Yet, the brutalities experienced by First Nations women continue in the present. Aboriginal women are at much greater risk of being the victims of homicide, rape and assault than non-Aboriginal women. They are 11 times more likely to die from an assault than non-indigenous women, and 32 times more likely to be hospitalized because of family violence. Three in five Aboriginal and Torres Strait Islander women have experienced physical or sexual violence by a male partner. When Aboriginal and Torres Strait Islander women go to authorities for support, they are often ignored or subject to further violence. This violence also extends to acts mandated by the government, including the high rates of incarceration of First Nations women,

deaths in custody, removal of children from their families, enhanced policing surveillance of indigenous communities and police inaction, and lack of public support when First Nations women are subject to violent assault and death.

Political mobilization

In response to continued gendered violence, First Nations women have mobilized by taking to the streets in rallies in capital cities and regional towns across Australia. On 15 March 2021, indigenous organizers, politicians and citizenry joined forces with the Women's March 4 Justice. The 110,000-strong March 4 Justice protests were organized following the perceived lack of government response to reports that a young white female political staffer was raped by a senior male colleague in Australia's parliament house in Canberra and the emergence of historical allegations of rape by the country's attorney-general. The protests tapped into a greater push for gender equality in Australia, particularly among First Nations women. Indigenous women joined the marches in solidarity for justice and change for women and to highlight the disproportionate impacts that sexual violence has on First Nations women. Aboriginal women are all too often erased from the mainstream feminist movement and discussions of domestic violence despite their

efforts to be included in political conversations. Through their powerful advocacy, Aboriginal feminists are helping to keep the voices of First Nations women at the centre of conversations about violence against women and equality.

First Nations Aboriginal people in Australia are incarcerated at a higher rate than any other group in the world.

Inspiring and shaping women's struggles in Chiapas

The Zapatista Army for National Liberation (EZLN) emerged in 1983 as an indigenous resistance organization in the southern Mexican state of Chiapas. In 1994, the Zapatistas rose up against the Mexican government. They gained control of substantial territory in Chiapas, which they govern to the present day through non-violent resistance.

A key aspect of the EZLN's ideology is gender equality. Female Zapatistas make up 40 per cent of the EZLN. Before the Zapatistas, indigenous women in Chiapas were often pushed into arranged marriages at a very young age. Women were generally encouraged to have a large number of children. As a result, they found themselves limited to the domestic sphere and unable to be a part of public decision-making. After the uprising, the EZLN advanced the Women's Revolutionary Law as a set of 10 laws that focused on women's rights in education, work, healthcare, marriage, children, violence, and political and military participation. As women like Comandante Ramona and Major Ana Maria became prominent political leaders, educators, healthcare workers and members of economic co-operatives, they began to shape the movement and advance gender reforms.

The Zapatistas have given important visibility to their efforts through workshops and social media, including bringing thousands of women together for the Zapatistas' 'First International Gathering of Women Who Struggle' in March 2018. Men assisted with cooking, cleaning and childcare duties to enable women to freely participate.

ABOVE: *At the Zapatista International Gathering of Women, signs welcome women and instruct men that they are prohibited from entering.*

LEFT: *Women's organizing led to the banning of alcohol and drugs in Zapatista territories, which women say has helped significantly reduce domestic violence and poverty.*

Indian women are no strangers to powerful protests. India has seen a wave of protests in response to sexual violence against women. In conservative Hindu beliefs, menstruating women are represented as unclean and barred from participating in certain religious rituals. Bollywood films still often promote stereotypes of women as sexualized and submissive. These combined popular culture and religious representations contribute to a perception among some of women as subordinate. That many people in Kerala disagreed with the Supreme Court decision to allow women into the temple suggests that bottom-up religious and social reform is needed.

India's *Vanitha Mathil* ('Women's Wall')

On 1 January 2019, one of the biggest women's rights protests in India took place. Across India's southern state of Kerala, millions of women formed a 620-km- (385-mile-) long 'Women's Wall' – *Vanitha Mathil* in the local Malayalam language – to support women's rights to enter the Sabarimala temple: a sacred Hindu pilgrimage site. Many men lined up on the other side of the highway to show their support. Since 1991, the Hindu temple had banned all women of menstrual age, between 10 and 50 years old, from entering.

In September 2018, in a huge challenge to religious tradition, the Indian Supreme Court had ruled that women of all ages must be able to enter the temple, stating that 'where a man can enter, a woman can also go. What applies to a man, applies to a woman.' However, attempts by women to enter the temple met with violent protests from mobs of male conservative devotees. Some women were shoved, others stoned, and none was able to make it inside, despite police protection and legal orders. In many of Kerala's towns, mobs set buses ablaze, turning the temple area into a virtual war zone. The temple's authorities pushed back against the ruling, closing the temple to conduct a 'purification ritual'. In response, women of all ages stood shoulder to shoulder along Kerala's National Highway 66, which runs along India's western coast. Estimates place the Women's Wall at between 3.5 and 5 million women, the largest human chain formed solely of women in the world.

Silencing women's activism: saviour narratives and Afghan women

Around the world, women participate in social struggles in inspiring and innovative ways, but often there is a tendency for these efforts to be hidden from view. Sometimes the activism of women in non-Western countries is rendered particularly invisible. Women's rights movements and pro-feminist narratives have also been appropriated to serve the geopolitical interests of other countries.

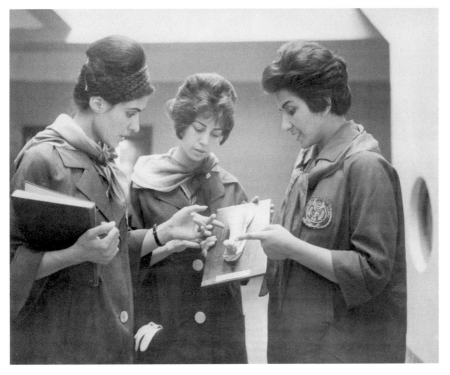

Kabul, the capital of Afghanistan, was a cosmopolitan hub in the 1960s and '70s. Prior to the return of Taliban rule, by the 1990s, women in the city eventually comprised 70 per cent of schoolteachers, 50 per cent of government workers and university students, and 40 per cent of doctors.

Since the Taliban's return to power in Afghanistan in 2021, much of the global media attention has focused on Afghani women's rights. The majority of Western media coverage pivots on a narrative that Euro-American military intervention expanded rights for Afghan women. During Taliban rule from 1996 to 2001, prior to the US NATO invasion, women could only go out in public if they were accompanied by a male guardian. They were banned from public education and participation in most workplaces and the government. The narrative of 'saving Afghan women' was front and centre in 2001 when then US President George W. Bush launched the 'war on terror', with US troops invading Afghanistan. His wife Laura publicly claimed that 'the fight against terrorism is also a fight for the rights and dignity of women'. In the UK, Tony Blair's government also used this justification as they sent in troops to join the international coalition and, among other concerns, 'give back a voice' to Afghan women under the Taliban regime.

It is certainly true that Afghan women faced incredible injustices under Taliban rule, but this kind of saviour narrative obscures the long histories of activism and political residence led by Afghan women through to the present day. Afghanistan is a multi-ethnic and largely tribal society, comprising numerous ethnolinguistic groups. Up to the 20th century, many nomadic ethnicities in Afghanistan upheld strict forms of gender segregation. These customs differed significantly between regions and religious and ethnic affiliations, but often barred women from public roles in society. Backed by influential women in the royal family, however, a succession of sovereigns in Afghanistan led a series of modernization reforms across the 1900s that gave women different possibilities for participating in Afghan society. This 'Young Afghan' nationalist movement included a series of social and legal reforms, such as the right for Afghan women to vote in 1920 (the same year as the USA), own property and access public education.

The gender segregations of conservative interpretation of sharia or Islamic law has not been without contestation from Afghani women.

Queen Soraya Tarzi

Queen Soraya Tarzi (1899–1968) was behind major social reforms for Afghan women. She founded the first school for girls in 1920, the first women's organization, *Anjuman-I Himayat-i-Niswan*, and the first women's magazine, *Irshad-e Naswan*. Tarzi advocated against mandated traditional dress codes and was known for ripping off her veil in public. This provoked tensions among women and men outside of the country's intellectual European-educated elite. She and her husband, King Amanullah Khan, were eventually overthrown and forced into exile by a traditionalist revolt.

Meena Keshwar Kamal

Meena Keshwar Kamal (1956–87) was an Afghan political and women's rights activist who founded the Revolutionary Association of the Women of Afghanistan (RAWA). She actively campaigned for women's rights to be placed at the top of the government's agenda and was opposed to foreign interference in Afghanistan. Her active social work and powerful advocacy against the Soviet rule of Afghanistan (1978–91) angered Russian and fundamentalist forces. She was assassinated in Pakistan by agents of Afghanistan's branch of the Russian secret service, the KGB. RAWA is still active as an organization. Their efforts focus on supporting education and healthcare for women, including underground schools for Afghan girls restricted from pursuing education.

Queen Soraya Tarzi pictured as a young woman during the 1920s, dressed in fashionable clothing of the time.

Meena Keshwar Kamal speaking in 1982.

Despite the Western narrative of liberation, RAWA and other Afghani activist groups have been extremely critical of the US-backed NATO invasion of Afghanistan. RAWA activists point to the high rate of casualties among the civilian population during the Western occupation, as well as the assaults on women by the US-backed Afghan government.

Afghan women are like sleeping lions, when awoken,
they can play a wonderful role in any social revolution.
– Meena Kamal

Afghanistan has one of the highest maternal mortality rates in the world. Women in remote rural areas often give birth without medical assistance. Midwives have therefore become indispensable to supporting childbirth in community-based facilities. Even after the Taliban took over the country again in 2021, midwives – and other female professionals – have used their specialized essential skills to leverage against possible restrictions to women's education and movement. In some regions, they have negotiated with elders to continue to practise and train students. In other places, the future is uncertain and women are carrying out their work below the radar.

DO MUSLIM WOMEN NEED SAVING?

In her book *Do Muslim Women Need Saving?* the anthropologist Lila Abu-Lughod (b. 1952) challenges simplistic stereotypes of female Muslim passivity; of women in the Middle East as victims of the veil, violent abuse and forced marriage. Veiling is often seen as a symbol of oppression in the West. However, those who wear veils do so for a variety of reasons that cannot be generalized as patriarchal oppression. Moreover, Western codes of dress and gendered fashion can also be read as systems of sexualized oppression. She argues that depicting Muslim women as oppressed erases gendered violence and oppression in the West. It also creates the idea that feminism is only a Western concept, nullifying the long histories of women's rights and leadership in Afghanistan.

As with women of any nationality, Afghan women cannot be generalized as fixed groups. They have a plurality of socio-economic and ethnic identities, and religious and non-religious backgrounds.

Chapter
5 CHALLENGING CONTEXTS

From the violence of slavery and battling discrimination to experiences of war, women are no strangers to navigating adversities. Through a myriad of ways, women find the means to overcome situations that threaten their lives. This includes asserting the right to live, work and love as they choose.

A candlelight march for world peace by Aa Aadmi Party (AAP) members in Gurgaon, India on 28 February 2022, four days after the Russian invasion of Ukraine.

Conflict involves and affects men and women differently. The dominant image of women in war is still that of victims. Certainly, for women, warfare and conflict frequently results in increased vulnerability to sexual exploitation. The hyper-masculinities of militarization increase violent attitudes, making women targets of sexual violence and rape. This leaves traumatizing psychological and physical effects, and destroys families and communities. Often, women are also faced with greater responsibilities, such as becoming breadwinners as well as the caregiving expectations of supporting a family. On the one hand, conflicts can enable women to access once male-dominated areas: becoming heads of households and securing financial independence. On the other hand, this comes with the drastic human costs of warfare. Whether conflicts result in women's empowerment or violent backlashes against them also depends on family backgrounds and socio-economic contexts. In some regions, the gender norms in place still obstruct women's access to education, resources and social, economic and political participation.

Counter to stereotypical images of women as passive victims of war, they also have complex experiences as fighters, survivors and protectors. Women are increasingly playing important roles in peacebuilding, too; at times, drawing on constructions

Ukrainian refugees on Lviv railway station on 7 March 2022 waiting for a train to escape the ongoing war.

of femininity as mothers and carers to humanize conflict and advance peace and prosperity. Too often, we hear little of these crucial efforts of women to bridge deep divides and mend communities, where women have been anything but passive bystanders of war. Since the conflict broke out in Syria in 2011, the country has experienced unprecedented devastation and displacement. Rajaa Altalli is co-founder of the NGO the Center for Civil Society and Democracy in Syria and a member of the Syrian Women's Advisory Board to the United Nations. Her work focuses on strengthening women's inclusion in Syria's formal peace process and pushing for stable political transitions.

Like Altalli, women around the world are instrumental in advancing peacemaking strategies across conflict lines. This chapter looks at women's experiences in challenging contexts, including the violence of slavery and struggles for LGBTQ+ equality. By consider gender as a system of power that is reinforced and resisted, we can better understand women's changing and diverse experiences in the contemporary world.

Rajaa Altalli speaks during an event recognizing the ongoing war crimes in Syria co-hosted by the US Holocaust Memorial Museum and House Committee on Foreign Affairs on 11 March 2020.

Women in slavery: the gender of violence

The transatlantic slave trade was a period of extreme violence from the 16th to 19th centuries. People, largely from Central and West Africa, were captured, enslaved and transported to the Americas to work on European plantations. Between 12 and 12.8 million Africans were shipped across the Atlantic under intensely brutal conditions. Millions perished during and after the voyages, as well as during the raids, conflicts and transportation involved in bringing people to the coast for sale to European traders. European colonialists created hierarchies by classifying people based on phenotype, especially skin colour, placing themselves at the top. This fabricated framework connected people's appearances with misconceptions about their intellect, physical abilities and overall worth. Such racial hierarchies were used to justify colonial domination, transatlantic slavery and the infliction of violence on populations.

Along with racial imperialism, sexism was also a major tool of social and political governance imposed by white colonizers. This had an enormous impact on enslaved Black women. The slave trade focused primarily on the importation of Black men as labourers. Black women slaves were not ranked as highly. However, women in Africa also became targets for white male slavers, and were generally sold into domestic work in the American colonies. They were branded with hot irons on board the boats, often beaten and subjected to extreme violence and abuse. Slave traders attempted to destroy people's dignity, including erasing their names from documentation, dispersing them so that no common language existed, and instilling regimes of terror so that there would be no signs of African heritage. African women faced great brutality, not just because of their sexuality but also because they would probably be working intimately with a white family. Since Black women were seen as marketable housekeepers, cooks and nurses, slave traders wanted to ensure that they would passively submit to a white family's will, and hence would be more 'sellable'.

On plantations, Black men were primarily exploited as labourers in the fields. Few Black men worked as domestics in the white household, unless as butlers, who held a higher status than maids. Black women were also exploited as labourers in the fields, and subject to violent assault and sexual exploitation. Labouring in the fields was a role deemed as 'masculine' in colonial American society; in the eyes of colonial white Americans, only degraded women worked in the fields. The kind of masculinization Black women experienced thus wholly degraded them as the lowest of humanity. It was these realities of extreme dehumanization – and their continued legacies – that Sojourner Truth spoke to in her powerful speech, 'Ain't I A Woman' (1851).

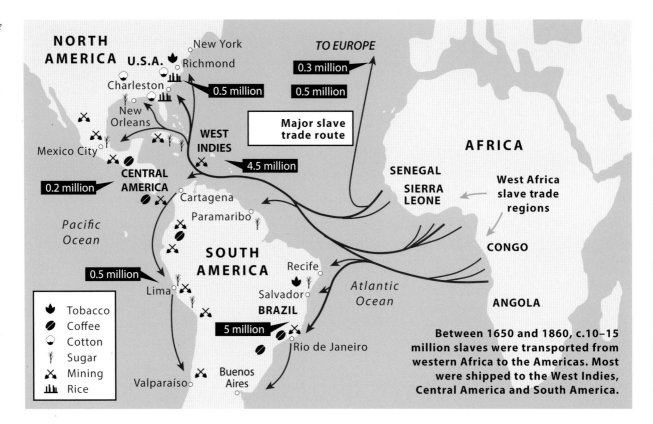

The slave trade from Africa to the Americas, 1650–1860.

NORTH AMERICA U.S.A.
New York
Richmond
Charleston
New Orleans
Mexico City
WEST INDIES
CENTRAL AMERICA
Cartagena
Paramaribo
Pacific Ocean
SOUTH AMERICA
Recife
Salvador
Lima
BRAZIL
Atlantic Ocean
Rio de Janeiro
Valparaíso
Buenos Aires

TO EUROPE
0.3 million
0.5 million
0.5 million
0.5 million
4.5 million
0.2 million
0.5 million
5 million

Major slave trade route

AFRICA
SENEGAL
SIERRA LEONE
West Africa slave trade regions
CONGO
ANGOLA

Between 1650 and 1860, c.10–15 million slaves were transported from western Africa to the Americas. Most were shipped to the West Indies, Central America and South America.

Tobacco
Coffee
Cotton
Sugar
Mining
Rice

Maria W. Stewart

Black women found many ways of fighting back against the horrendous conditions of enslavement and plantation life. There are accounts during the so-called 'middle passage' across the Atlantic of women rising up in resistance. On board the *Thomas* in 1797, for instance, a group of women were released on deck to exercise and eat. Once on deck, they seized guns from the unlocked armoury and overpowered the crew. They released the enslaved men on board and took control of the ship. Although they were eventually recaptured, this event shows the powerful resistance of women in unimaginable conditions of enslavement.

What's more, even in slavery, many women sustained cultural practices, such as storytelling, music-making, dancing, preparing food or herbal remedies and different ritual procedures. This ensured that they could retain a sense of self and oppose the slavery system that tried to make them anonymous, voiceless and without cultural identity.

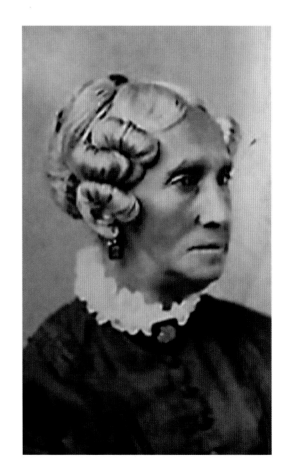

Maria W. Stewart (1803–79) was a Black abolitionist, feminist, author and educator who heavily influenced Truth, Frederick Douglass and Frances Watkins Harper, among others. She had a significant public speaking career that saw her calling for resistance against slavery, oppression and exploitation.

The Garifuna are descendants of Africans who escaped slavery and Indigenous Carib peoples of the Lesser Antilles. Many Garifuna still live in Honduras, Belize and Guatemala, continuing to maintain a rich Afro-indigenous culture.

A modern woodcut depicting Queen Nanny.

Queen Nanny

Originally from Ghana, Queen Nanny (1686–1733) was a Jamaican heroine and emblematic figure of female resistance against slavery. Nanny was from the Ashanti tribe of Ghana, whose women were well trained in fighting battles and revered. Along with her five brothers, Nanny fled the harsh conditions of the Jamaican plantation into the mountains. She founded a Maroon ('Maroons' were slaves in the Americas who escaped and formed independent settlements) village in the Blue Mountains of eastern Jamaica, known as 'Nanny Town'. There, they lived by cattle breeding, agriculture, hunting and barter with other Maroon settlements. As leader, she trained others in guerilla warfare to fend off the British colonialists. She also helped more than 1,000 enslaved people escape to the Maroon community. As the community grew, the British colonial forces became more violent in their attacks. During one of the battles, Nanny was killed. Her brother, Cudjoe, eventually signed a peace treaty with the British, which granted the Maroons 500 acres (200 ha) of land for settlement, land that was known as 'New Nanny Town'. Nanny is still hailed for her role in protecting the Black community and fighting slavery.

Phyllis Wheatley

Phillis Wheatley (1753–84) was born in Senegal and sold into slavery as a young girl. She was transported to North America and bought by the Wheatley family in Boston. Quickly learning to read and write, she soon gained national acclaim for her poetry, which focused on themes of freedom and slavery, subtly drawing attention to the use of religion to disenfranchise Black people. At the time, few Black women had the opportunity to learn to read and write like Wheatley; for her, the act of writing poetry was one way of asserting humanity. According to prevalent white views, Black women did not feel emotions or pain. Wheatley used the European format of poetry to challenge these racist beliefs and criticize white supremacy.

Harriet Tubman

Harriet Tubman (1822–1913), known as 'Moses of Her People', was an American political activist and abolitionist. She was born into slavery in Maryland, during which time she experienced extreme violence, being beaten and whipped by her various white owners as a child. At one point, she experienced a head wound so great that she suffered from dizziness and insomnia for the rest of her life. In 1849, Tubman escaped to Philadelphia, subsequently returning to rescue her family. Travelling in extreme secrecy by night, she gradually helped more relatives and dozens of other enslaved people to escape the state to freedom in Northern states and Canada.

A *sketch of Phyllis Wheatley from the frontispiece of one of her books,* Poems on Various Subjects, Religious and Moral, 1773.

A *perhaps uncharacteristically relaxed Harriet Tubman photographed* c.1868/9.

The Underground Railroad

The Underground Railroad was a secret network of passages and safe houses used by enslaved African Americans to escape to free Northern states, Canada, Mexico and Caribbean islands that were not part of the slave trade. The network was supported by Black and white abolitionists and other sympathizers, who collectively helped people escape the violent conditions of slavery. As a 'conductor', Tubman played a significant part in its operations. During the American Civil War (1861–5), fought between the Union and Confederate Armies around the status of slavery, Tubman took on a command role in Union Army anti-slavery operations.

There were various safe houses along the Underground Railroad, which were often indicated by quilts hanging outside. These were embedded with secret codes, whereby the shapes and motifs of the design told people in the know about the area's dangers or where to safely go next. This use of the art of quilting became a powerful means of supporting resistance among largely Black but also some white women artisans.

The Underground Railroad network c.1860.

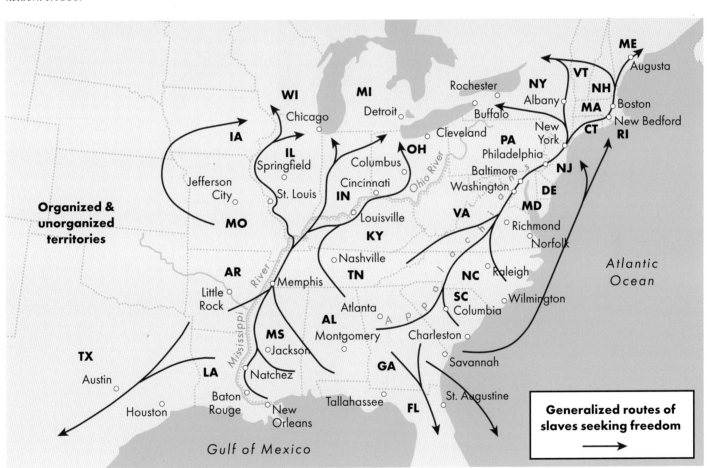

A quilt of the kind that was displayed by safe houses on the Underground Railroad.

Shoo Fly design = people who might help escaping enslaved people.

Bear Paw motifs = follow an animal trail to find food and water.

Log cabin quilt blocks = directed you to a safe house for shelter.

Enduring impacts of slavery

A number of modern writers have considered the enduring legacy of slavery on the experiences of Black women.

bell hooks

The trailblazing Black feminist bell hooks (1952–2021) wrote extensively on the marginalization of Black women. In her book *Ain't I A Woman? Black Women and Feminism* (1981) – a title borrowed from Sojourner Truth – hooks traces how the devaluation of Black womanhood is the direct result of the histories of sexual exploitation of Black women during slavery. She questions the claim of feminists to speak for all women, arguing that working-class and Black women's unique experiences have been pushed to the margins. hooks used all lowercase letters in her name (a pen name that was her great-grandmother's) to prioritize a focus on the substance of her words, not her personal qualities or individuality.

bell hooks photographed during a publicity tour in 1999. She said: 'Don't take my picture so close up. That's what white photographers do.'

Kimberlé Crenshaw

The American feminist legal scholar Kimberlé Crenshaw (b. 1959) coined the term 'intersectionality' to show how discrimination can occur in multiple systems of power at once, such as race, gender and class. She used the example of Black women being discriminated against, not just as Black people, not just as women, but as *Black women*. Intersectionality describes how these multiple identities collide in people's lives through forms of discrimination or privilege.

RIGHT: *Civil rights advocate Kimberlé Williams Crenshaw speaks onstage at the 2018 Women's March Los Angeles at Pershing Square on 20 January 2018 in Los Angeles, California.*

Intersectionality

This concept of 'intersectionality' is indebted to the writings of women such as the French-Martinique writer Paulette Nardal (1896–1985), the Trinidad and Tobago activist-journalist Claudia Jones (1915–64) and the Jamaican activist and writer Una Marson (1905–65). Each of these women wrote incredible analyses of the intersections between colonialism, race, gender and class long before theories of intersectionality were popularized.

LEFT: *Claudia Jones moved to the UK in the 1950s, where she founded Britain's first major Black newspaper, the* West Indian Gazette, *and was a founder of the Notting Hill Carnival, the second-largest annual carnival in the world.*

Slavery by another name: the new Jim Crow

The American writer, legal scholar and civil rights activist Michelle Alexander (b. 1967) refers to 'the new Jim Crow' to trace how the current system of mass incarceration of people of colour in the USA is an extension of slavery. The Jim Crow laws were a series of state and local laws beginning in the 1870s that enforced racial segregation in the southern USA. It is commonly said that the civil rights era of the 1960s ended systemic racial discrimination. However, Alexander argues that new convictions over low-level drug offences have become a tool of discrimination and oppression against people of colour. Not only does the USA have the highest rate of incarceration in the world, but the overwhelming majority of people in US prisons are African American men. Alexander shows how prisons continue a racial caste system that bars them from basic civil and human rights: very similar to Jim Crow. In other countries such as the UK, the percentage of Black people imprisoned is far higher than other groups.

Others have taken up Alexander's argument, referring to the 'New Jane Crow', looking at the ways in which poor Black and LatinX women experience extreme institutional violence in the criminal justice system and are structurally trapped from advancing, with little to no resources. Many of these racial and ethnic disparities are repeated and experienced by minority and persecuted communities around the world. It is this that in part explains why #BlackLivesMatter attracted such a huge following globally as a rallying cry for equality.

Michelle Alexander pictured in 2013.

Angela Davis

Angela Davis (b. 1944) is a major leader of the prison abolition movement. She also argues that the US prison system is a new form of slavery, disproportionately affecting African Americans. In her work with the grassroots organization Critical Resistance, she focuses on education and building engaged communities to tackle social challenges currently dealt with through state policing institutions.

Angela Davis in 2018.

#BLACKLIVESMATTER

Alicia Garza, Patrisse Cullors and Opal Tometi are the three social justice organizers who created the Black-centred movement building project #BlackLivesMatter. It was started in response to the acquittal of the killer of the young African American teenager Trayvon Martin in Florida in 2012. The project has since become a powerful member-led global network with over 40 chapters to protest against the systemic racism that overwhelmingly affects Black communities around the world.

Mariame Kaba

Mariame Kaba is an American prison industrial complex (PIC) abolitionist and grassroots organizer. The PIC describes the government, corporate, non-governmental agencies and other individuals that benefit from forms of incarceration, including prisons, detention facilities, policing, surveillance and punishment-driven and corrections technologies. Like Davis, Kaba focuses on building up community services rather than reforming policing. She founded Project NIA, an organization centred on ending youth incarceration.

Mariame Kaba.

Environmental racism

The legacies of slavery are not just evident in prison systems but also in other structural impediments to people's physical and economic mobility, voice and opportunity. Environmental racism is a concept used to describe forms of systemic racism whereby communities of colour are disproportionately burdened with health hazards that force them to live near sources of toxic waste, such as landfills, industrial works, sewage sites, mines, power stations, major roads and other toxic emitters.

In South Africa, for example, environmental racism overwhelmingly affects the lives of low-income Black communities. During the colonial (1652–1931) and apartheid regimes (1948–91), Black South Africans experienced extreme racial segregation at the hands of white (majority Dutch) South Africans. To this day, most Black South Africans live in the most damaged and polluted areas near steel mills, coal-fired power stations and waste sites. Many also struggle for access to clean water and air and basic services. In response, African ecofeminist activists have mobilized against mining corporations and government agencies, fiercely defending their rights to livelihoods, health and well-being.

Women in South Africa protest against the activities of a number of energy and metal extraction companies.

Women and warfare

From the beginning of written records, documentary evidence chronicles the significant and diverse experiences of women in warfare. The idea that women are just victims of war and naturally oppose it obscures the complexities of how women take sides and risks, take up arms and wage war. Nor is being male synonymous with aggression or the desire to dominate or commit violence against others. Historically, women have held major roles in battlefields and on home fronts. They have fought ruthlessly, lead soldiers into combat, defended home regions and engaged in special espionage operations. Yet to this day, the involvement of women in warfare is often rendered invisible.

That said, it is true that women are far less prominent than men in combat zones. They still comprise a lower percentage of the military in most countries, although the number is increasing: 30 per cent in Eritrea, 25 per cent in China, 15.7 per cent in the USA, 15 per cent in France and 11 per cent in the UK. Earlier hypotheses have explained these disparities as fundamental differences between the sexes surrounding strength and aggression. Others have argued that the pattern of male-dominated warfare is rooted deep in our evolutionary past. According to aspects of this hypothesis, our ancestors decided that the risks of dying or injury were too great for women to take on, as they are more important to human procreation. Male competition over obtaining resources and opportunities for reproduction – what biologists term 'sexual selection' – might also have resulted in a male bias in participation in war. Studies now suggest that culture plays a huge role in shaping the 'appropriate' role of women in warfare too. In many regions of the world, aggressiveness is encouraged among young boys, with masculinity and soldiering fundamentally linked. And yet these initial conditions could have been quite different, resulting in majority female-dominated wars. This is certainly the case in some animal societies, such as spotted hyenas, where only females engage in inter-group conflicts.

THE VIOLENCE OF WAR

Critics argue that the question is not whether women can fight, but whether they *should*. Instead, we must examine the huge costs of war and cultural constructions that seek to glorify the military and the 'warrior hero', often for political populism. These representations produce assumptions that non-combatants are 'weak', that war is 'normal' or even that it is 'a good thing'.

The People's Liberation Army Ground Force (PLAGF) of China is the largest army in the world, with 1.6 million troops. Although women have had significant roles in warfare across Chinese history, they make up just 4.5 per cent of the PLA. This is a stark contrast to the North Korean military, where women comprise 40 per cent of the North Korean People's Ground Force: the highest proportion in the world.

In China, in unsettled ancient times from the Shang dynasty (1600–1046BCE) to the Warring States period (246–221BCE), when rival Chinese states viciously battled for territorial dominance, women led armies. Like their counterparts in different times and places, they defended borders against invasions and organized the defence of cities under siege. They also helped defend and establish new dynasties, trained armies, and led and limited peasant uprisings. Long before legendary Amazonian warriors rode into battle against the Greeks and Persians, General Fu Hao (c.1200BCE) was the most powerful military leader of the Shang dynasty. With an army of 13,000 soldiers under her command, she led the earliest large-scale ambush recorded in Chinese history against the neighbouring state of Ba. Warfare in China had previously been a primarily masculine activity, making Fu Hao's story particularly remarkable. Like many female warriors, she defied societal standards and laws in order to fight. However, she was not alone: archaeological investigations have revealed that in fact hundreds of women participated in the military during this era.

A commanding statue of the powerful Shang general Fu Hao.

War beyond combat

Conflict is often represented as only occurring on battlefields, but this is very much not the case. The 'political' takes place in spaces that are often imagined as purely economic or private. In many places, women have played important roles on home fronts, stepping into manufacturing and agricultural positions to ensure the running of societies. At the time of World War I (1914–18), most women in the participating countries were still barred from voting or taking on military combat roles. For many women, the war was an opportunity to support their country. It was also a time to obtain social and economic roles that they had been previously denied. Some women were employed in munitions factories and in vital construction work. Others accompanied armies on combat missions, taking on frontline support roles as nurses, ambulance drivers, doctors, cleaners, cooks and translators. These roles expanded across many participating countries during World War II.

A popular British poster from World War I contrasts the anguish of women and children left behind with the positive message to their men to sign up.

WHY IS WAR SUCH A MALE-DOMINATED ACTIVITY?

Killing is not a natural act for either gender, yet the vast majority of soldiers in today's standing armies are male. To encourage people to fight, cultures develop gender constructions that connect ideas of 'manhood' with toughness. To ensure that essential roles on the home front are performed, marketing campaigns equate femininity with domesticity and non-combat roles. To this day, women in combat still battle accusations of a reckless lack of maternalism or are stripped of their femininity.

LEFT: *Members of the Soviet 588th Night Bomber Regiment were nicknamed the 'Night Witches' by German soldiers because of the whooshing sound of their planes. Rumours spread that the women had the night vision of a cat. The name soon became a badge of honour because of the pilots' military prowess as the most highly decorated unit in the Soviet Air Force during World War II.*

BELOW: *'Rosie the Riveter' was an iconic image of World War II in the USA, used to encourage women to work in factories and shipyards serving the military industries. Male conscription left significant gaps in the industrial labour force. Galvanised by the US government's Rosie the Riveter campaign, many women entered professions from which they had previously been barred. However, female workers often earned less than 50 per cent of the wages paid to their male counterparts.*

The 'Night Witches'

The Soviet Union, in particular, mobilized women in frontline units in the Red Army. The so-called 'Night Witches' were the first women military pilots of the 20th century to directly engage in enemy combat. Organized by Major Marina Raskova, the 588th Regiment was an entirely female division, including the ground crews, navigators and support staff. Eventually, there was a total of three all-female air force units, as well as women pilots in mixed divisions.

Cultural constructions of women and war

During the world wars, the massive conscription of men created a shortage of available workers. Campaigns such as 'Rosie the Riveter' encouraged women in the USA to volunteer for wartime services and work in factories and shipyards on the home front. Similar images have been used in countries around the world, such as propaganda posters from Japan. These posters solidify constructions of women as different to men and having non-combatant roles. On the other hand, government posters and commercial advertising have, at different moments, depicted women as combatants, as is the case with some posters from Vietnam. Such diverse representations reveal the power that media and cultural propaganda have on our understandings of what it means to be 'a woman' or 'a man'.

Propaganda posters from Japan (left) and Vietnam (right) encourage different roles for women in war.

Pacifism and peace in the world wars

Some women also actively lobbied against the world wars. After World War I erupted in 1914, many women's organizations involved themselves in peace activities. These pacifist approaches went against the dominant political populism of the time, which advocated for warlike foreign policy. In fact, many women who supported pacifism, such as through international mediation, did so in the face of extreme marginalization. In consequence, some feminist divisions publicly supported the war in order to strengthen their own positions and avoid marginalizing women's rights still further.

In the UK, the picture was complex: prominent suffragists like Emmeline and Christabel Pankhurst and Millicent Fawcett supported the war effort and many feminists at the time took part in shaming young men into joining the armed services. Known as the 'White Feather Brigade', they would hand out white feathers symbolizing cowardice to any man who did not wear a uniform or was known not to

INTERNATIONALISTS AND ANTIMILITARISTS

As with many other participating countries, in the USA all men between the ages of 21 and 30 were required to register for military service in World War I. The No Conscription League was an anarchist organization in New York focused on challenging the draft and supporting those who refused conscription. The organizers, Emma Goldman and Alexander Berkman, were charged with conspiracy to 'induce persons not to register', sentenced to two years in prison and then deported back to Russia.

Hungarian activist Rosika Schwimmer (1877–1948)

have enlisted. In contrast, a number of other suffragists, such as Sylvia Pankhurst, Emily Hobhouse, Helena Swanwick and Catherine Marshall, were proponents of non-violence. They argued that militarism was a form of patriarchy and that handing out white feathers implicated women in the raising of armies. Some of these women saw their actions – whether in support of or against the war effort – as a way of using their sexual power, although anti-war feminists argued that handing out white feathers reinforced tropes of feminine weakness, drawing on a patriotic appeal that aligned masculinity with military service. It is interesting to note that the White Feather Brigade was actually started by a man, Admiral Charles Penrose Fitzgerald, a war supporter in Folkestone who thought that public humiliation by women would push men to join the war.

Many notable women promoted a specific transnational role in peace. For example, the Hungarian anti-war activist Rosika Schwimmer (1877–1948) convinced the American auto magnate Henry Ford to back and allow her to lead a 'Peace Ship' from New Jersey to Europe. The goal of the ship was

The passenger steamship Oscar II, *or the 'Peace Ship', leaving New Jersey on 4 December 1915.*

Jane Addams, c.1926.

to convince people in neutral European countries to advance international mediation and prevent further loss of life. Schwimmer had also been part of similar efforts in the Hague International Congress of Women earlier that year, which focused on involving women in parliamentary debates and settling international disputes through diplomacy and arbitration. But like the Hague Congress, the Peace Ship was largely ridiculed by the predominately male sensationalist press. Schwimmer herself was denied US citizenship because of her pacifist views, revealing just how ingrained militarization had become to the American national psyche.

The Woman's Peace Party, founded in the USA in 1915 in response to World War I, also had a specific focus on peace as 'a woman's issue'. The organizers saw women's participation in international politics as crucial to ending global conflict. International relations feminists argued that women contributed an important perspective as women often suffer disproportionately in war. The Woman's Peace Party used quite different tactics to previous peace organizations that worked mostly behind the scenes to influence policy. Instead, they employed direct action through public demonstrations in order to build popular support for peace. The Peace Party is still in existence, now known as the Women's International League for Peace and Freedom (WILPF).

The social reformer and co-founder of the American Civil Liberties Union (ACLU) Jane Addams (1860–1935) was the first American woman to be awarded the Nobel Peace Prize, in 1931. Addams ran the renowned women's settlement house Hull House in Chicago, which provided social and education opportunities for the working-class, and predominately migrant, population in the neighbourhood. Addams spoke out about intersecting concerns of aggressive policing, women's labour exploitation, minority rights, social inequality and conflict. She chaired the Hague International Congress of Women that Schwimmer took part in. She tried unsuccessfully to persuade the US President Woodrow Wilson to mediate between warring European countries. Addams was in vocal

LEFT: *The Women's Peace Parade on 29 August 1914 marked the established of the Woman's Peace Party (WPP) just four months later. Held in New York City, it featured more than 1,500 women marching down Fifth Avenue in a silent procession.*

BELOW: *Referred to as the 'Mother of Feminism', Gloria Steinem (b. 1934) was a leader and spokesperson for the American women's liberation movements throughout the 1960s and '70s – and continued to be a trailblazer for feminism well into the 21st century.*

opposition when the USA instead chose to enter World War I. As a result, she was labelled as a dangerous radical and a threat to American security. Nevertheless, later presidents, such as Calvin Coolidge, supported the anti-war policies of Addams and the WILPF (of which Addams was president). She was widely recognized as a hugely influential figure of the US Progressive Era (1896–1916).

The mediation campaign of the peace movement during World War I left a major legacy in international relations, in particular the importance of citizen diplomacy and the push for peace to be defined as a human right. Feminist pacifists also created a precedent for women's leadership in political protest.

Anarcha-feminism: Mujeres Libres and *milicianas* in Spain

Anarcha-feminism began as a political philosophy in the late 1800s. It combined critiques of capitalism and state power with critiques of patriarchy. Many theorists and activists, such as Emma Goldman (1869–1940), spoke out about how women's inferiority is embedded in – and essential to – the reproduction of the capitalist system: such as through unwaged women's domestic work, low-paid jobs as secretaries and factory workers, and the glorification of motherhood.

Spain was a fermenting ground for anarcha-feminist concerns to be implemented. In pre-Civil War Spain, women were extremely subordinated to men, owing largely to the heavy influence of the Catholic Church. Founded in late 1936 at the start of the Spanish Civil War (1936–39), Mujeres Libres (Free Women), was an anarcho-feminist organization with a massive following. The organization focused on combating the rampant sexism across Spain, seeking to end the 'triple enslavement of women, to ignorance, to capital, and to men' – barriers that prevented women from participating on an equal playing field in bettering society.

The vast majority of the organization's members were working-class women. In just over two years of existence – it didn't survive the fall of the Spanish Republic – Mujeres Libres membership numbered between 20,000 and 60,000 women. The organizers did not see Mujeres Libres as feminist, which they rejected as existing for the middle-class – or bourgeois – associations. But the theory and practice of their focus was certainly anarcho-feminism. They recognized how women's oppression is gender specific and the need to overcome it through autonomous female struggle.

Anarcha-feminism – an anti-authoritarian and anti-capitalist philosophy united by the struggle against women's subordination. Anarcha-feminism is intersectional in that anarcha-feminists argue that women's liberation needs to be fought alongside struggles against other forms of oppression embedded in capitalist patriarchal society, such as homophobia, transphobia, racism and class issues.

Mujeres Libres took a different approach to the mainstream anarchist movement. The organizers knew that more active steps were required than revolution alone to achieve equality.

Amparo Poch y Gascón.

Lucia Sánchez Saornil.

To this end, Mujeres Libres focused on supporting women's involvement in the political sphere. At this time, Spain still had very low literacy levels. Education and women's illiteracy were at the forefront of their activities. Women activists set up rural collectives where they organized literacy programmes and women-only social clubs and newspapers, and provided classes for women on subjects from sociology to economics, as well as instructions on birth control. They set up 'flying day-care centres' where women with childcare responsibilities could leave their children so that they could attend labour union meetings.

Prominent leaders in Mujeres Libres

Amparo Poch y Gascón

Amparo Poch y Gascón (1902–68) was a Spanish anarchist, activist, pacifist and doctor, and director of social assistance at the Ministry of Health and Social Assistance. She promoted public health and women's sexuality and advocated for women's sexual freedom, including against sexual double standards that judge sexual behaviour differently for women and men. She helped establish support centres for women involved in sex work. There, they could receive healthcare, psychosocial support and professional training in other career sectors.

Lucia Sánchez Saorn

The Spanish poet, feminist and anarchist Lucia Sánchez Saornil (1895–1970) was another founder of Mujeres Libres. She wrote about LGBTQ sexuality, free love and the repressiveness of gender roles in Spain. This included rejecting female domesticity and the idea that motherhood and reproduction is synonymous with female identity. Saornil worked at a time when homosexuality was criminalized so often wrote under a male pen name – Luciano de San Saor – in order to freely explore themes of gay identity.

Federica Montseny

Federica Montseny (1905–94) was a Spanish intellectual, writer and anarchist who was the Minister of Health and Social Policy during the Second Spanish Republic of the Civil War (1931–39), serving in a coalition of left-wing anti-fascist groups known as 'the Popular Front'. She was the first female cabinet minister in Spain and one also of the first in Western Europe. She focused her work on transforming public health to support the poor and working class. She was one of the most powerful members of Mujeres Libres, advancing direct healthcare policy changes focused on women's rights. Montseny pushed for decentralized and locally responsive programmes so that changes could be more effectively implemented. However, some of the more militant anarchists criticized the compromises that anarchists like Montseny made as part of the Popular Front.

Emma Goldman

Emma Goldman (1869–1940) was an anarchist political organizer and writer. She was hugely influential in developing anarchist political philosophy in Europe and North America. Born in present-day Lithuania (then part of the Russian Empire), Goldman emigrated to the USA at a young age. She championed a range of social justice concerns, including free speech, gender and racial justice, birth control, free love, worker's rights and free universal education. Goldman saw suffrage as a useless cause, arguing that the middle-class women participating in the marches cared little about working-class women's issues.

Federica Montseny.

Emma Goldman.

Goldman's writings were very influential over the organizers of Mujeres Libres and other labour unions and anarchist federations across Spain. At the time of the Civil War, Goldman lived in the UK after her deportation to Russia for protesting against the American compulsory draft. She went to Spain following correspondence with Saornil and other activists, where she supported the Republicans in their battle against Franco's Nationalists. She assisted a number of organizations in their English-language campaigns, including the National Confederation of Labor (CNT) and the Iberian Anarchist Federation (FAI). She was later referred to as the 'spiritual mother' of the Spanish anarchist cause. When Franco gained victory in 1939, Goldman moved to Canada, where she helped secure political asylum and financial support for those leaving Spain from the Civil War.

The militianas *– or militiawomen – became Republican icons in the anti-fascist resistance against the Franco-led Nationalist side.*

Milicianas **and combat**

Mujeres Libres was active during the time of the Spanish Civil War, in which women had prominent combatant roles on the left-wing Republican side. Women played a major role in the front lines and in the armed rearguard, constituting the most substantial mass mobilization of women to fight on equal terms with men in Spanish history. Many organizers saw this social revolution as a way to advance women's liberation. Others, such as Poch y Gascón, were war resisters. During the Civil War, she was active in Orden del Olivo (The Order of the Olive Tree), which was the Spanish division of War Resisters' International.

The combat involvement of *milicianas* – militiawomen – denoted a change occurring in gender roles from socially accepted codes of behaviour. This only lasted a short time. With the defeat of the Republican side, many *milicianas* were imprisoned and tortured, with the *miliciana* phenomenon erased from history. The organizers of Mujeres Libres, and many of those involved in the push for women's liberation, were forced to go into exile in France and other countries. During the ensuing Franco dictatorship (1939–75), many of the advancements of Mujeres Libres were rolled back significantly, including female access to education. Nevertheless, the liberation ideology of women, born from stifling experiences, laid the bedrock for later powerful feminist movements in Spain following the end of the Franco dictatorship.

Women and peace: protesting against the horrors of war

Violence in warfare has been committed by, but also overwhelmingly experienced by, women. Toxic displays of masculinity often involve extreme targeted violence and domination over women. The impacts of war – including reduction in access to food and water, electricity and other basic services, loss of family members and increase in illness and disability – all heighten women's risks of assault and worsen women's labour conditions. As women are often disproportionately tasked with caregiving to children, partners, elders, the sick and disabled, worsening conditions for doing that work in wartime disproportionately affect their daily lives. In response, women have mobilized for peace, drawing on identities as mothers, sisters, wives and daughters. In so doing, they have been agents of change in advancing peace for their country's futures and inspiring others elsewhere.

Women of Liberia Mass Action for Peace

Liberia experienced two brutal back-to-back civil wars, from 1989 to 1997 then, after Charles Taylor was elected president, from 1999 to 2003. At least 250,000 people were killed, and many more were internally displaced or sought refuge in neighbouring regions and further afield. The Women of Liberia Mass Action for Peace movement was vital in helping to end Liberia's second civil war. Dressed in white, women participants became highly visible across Liberia's capital, Monrovia, fasting, singing and praying for peace. Thousands of women from diverse social and religious backgrounds joined the peaceful sit-ins, demanding that the fighting be resolved. A delegation of women from the movement, led by Leymah Gbowee (b. 1972), eventually succeeded into bringing then-president Charles Taylor and rebel leaders to talks in Ghana. During the peace process, they continued to pressure the warring sides to find a resolution. They staged a sit-in outside the Presidential Palace, where the talks took place, blocking the exits of the negotiating hall until the groups reached a consensus and signed the Accra Comprehensive Peace Agreement on 17 June 2003.

The women's movement continued a campaign of non-violent advocacy, including civic education and voter registration drives, until democratic elections were held two years later. In 2005, Ellen Johnson Sirleaf (b. 1938) was elected president of Liberia, becoming the first female head of state in an African country. Sirleaf went on to serve two full terms as president, putting through significant changes to advance gender equity. Gbowee has supported peacebuilding efforts and the work of women's organizations internationally.

BELOW: *Tawakkol Karman (left), Leymah Gbowee (centre) and Ellen Johnson Sirleaf (right) were awarded the Nobel Peace Prize in 2011 for their 'non-violent struggle for the safety of women and for women's rights to full participation in peace-building work'. Karman is a Yemeni journalist and human rights activist who advanced freedom for the press during the 2011 Yemeni uprising.*

LEFT: *In Northern Ireland, Betty Williams (1943–2020) and Mairead Corrigan-Maguire (b. 1944) received the Nobel Peace Prize in 1976 for their work in initiating Women for Peace, later the Community for Peace People. They dedicated their work to advancing peaceful resolutions of 'the Troubles' in Northern Ireland: a violent conflict between predominately Protestant unionists and Irish-nationalist Catholics (who wanted independence from Britain), which lasted from the 1960s to the Good Friday Agreement of 1998.*

The Greenham Common Women's Peace Camp in the UK was a sustained non-violent protest lasting from 1981 to 2000. This transformative action brought together more than 70,000 women to protest against nuclear armament outside the US Air Force's nuclear weapons storage facility at Greenham Common in Berkshire, England. It was one of the longest and largest feminist protests in recent years. Living together communally on such a massive scale was a powerful means of feminist consciousness-raising. For many women, it gave them the opportunity to live outside the control of men and the heterosexual family unit.

Baby strollers left at a railway station in Przemysl, Poland, for Ukrainians to use after fleeing the Russian invasion in February 2022.

When Russia invaded Ukraine in 2022, millions of people were forced to leave. In response, European countries came together to offer humanitarian aid and support. The vast majority of those leaving are women and children, as most Ukrainian men between the ages of 18 and 60 were banned from leaving the country, with the expectation that they might be called to fight. In a powerful gesture of solidarity, mothers from other countries left strollers lined with blankets and essential supplies at train stations and border crossings in Poland and Slovakia for Ukrainian parents arriving and seeking refuge.

Gendered inequities: period taboos and period poverty

Periods are a biological process experienced by the majority of women, non-binary and transgender individuals as part of their monthly cycle. Most people have normal vaginal bleeding for a few days as the lining of their uterus sheds. This menstrual cycle is a natural part of the reproductive system. Some cultures have period traditions that celebrate when an individual enters puberty as a coming-of-age event. In some regions of Japan, for instance, the family marks the occasion by eating a traditional dish called *sekihan* made of sticky rice and red beans. Among the Apache of North America, the Sunrise Dance is a significant female coming-of-age ceremony in the summer of a girl's first period. Over four days, the girl takes part in a number of ritual practices, including special dances to demonstrate her strength and transition to womanhood.

Periods are naturally experienced by a huge proportion of the world's population. Yet, in some societies, menstrual care is highly taboo. Menstruation is sometimes seen as embarrassing or unclean and suppressed from public and/or private conversation. A number of traditional religions even deem menstruation ritually unclean and ban women from participating in particular actions, such as the practice of *niddah* in Orthodox Judaism. In rural western Nepal, *chhaupadi* is a menstrual taboo that prohibits menstruating women from participating in everyday activities because they are considered impure. During this time, women are made to live in a makeshift dwelling or menstruation hut – often with minimal supplies and no menstrual protection or facilities for washing; *chhaupadi* has resulted in deaths from dehydration, animal attacks, smoke inhalation and pneumonia. It was made illegal in 2005 by the Supreme Court of Nepal, although it is still practised in some communities.

Menarche – the first menstrual period, which may be experienced at many different ages.

Indigenous Aboriginal rock art of two women dancing and menstruating from the Pilbara region of Western Australia.

The Native American Na'ii'ees or Sunrise Dance is a ritual re-enactment of the Apache Origin Myth held across four days in the summer following an Apache girl's first period. In it, the female participant personifies Changing Woman, the first woman and respected mother of her people.

In Nepalese chhaupadi rituals, young girls are sent to menstruation huts for fear of their impurity. These are often poorly built and may be cow sheds made from grass, mud and sticks. Such traditional practices of isolation are widespread but are facing challenges from women rebelling against the tradition, encouraging each other to see periods as a form of power rather than shame and constraining to their autonomy.

Sekihan (赤飯) is a festive dish served on special occasions in Japan, made of sticky steamed rice with red azuki beans.

Period poverty

Period poverty describes the inability to afford or access adequate menstrual products, toilets, running water, hand-washing facilities, menstrual hygiene education and waste management. It means that an individual could be faced with using makeshift menstrual protection, including unhygienic newspapers, socks, old clothes or rags, and/or prevented from attending school, going to work or engaging in everyday life. For many people, period products are a luxury item that they cannot afford. Those living in low-income countries are disproportionately affected, particularly in places where basic sanitation services are unavailable. Those with disabilities, living in conflict- or natural-disaster-affected areas also experience compounded obstacles to menstrual hygiene. This can lead to physical health risks from the introduction of bacteria, such as reproductive and urinary tract infections. Keeping the same tampon in for multiple days in a row puts users at risk of life-threatening toxic shock syndrome caused by bacteria releasing harmful toxins.

These limitations are not just experienced in countries in the Global South. Bloody Good Period, a British charity that provides free period products and fights

The drive towards a unified effort to alleviate inequalities in the provision of, and access to, period products has grown more powerful in recent years.

for menstrual equity, found that one in 10 young women in the UK cannot afford period products. Thanks to the work of the British activist Amika George (b. 1999) and her fellow campaigners, state schools in England now receive government funding to provide free sanitary products to students, including girls, non-binary and transgender learners who have periods. A number of supermarkets and healthcare retailers, such as Morrisons, Boots and Superdrug, also provide free pads and tampons to those who need them.

THE TAMPON TAX OR 'PINK TAX'

In some countries, including some US states, menstrual products are taxed as luxury 'non-essential' items. This places an additional burden on those who menstruate, making tampons or pads that are essential for everyday life unaffordable for some. Many people resort to unsafe materials to manage their periods because they cannot obtain free menstrual products in their schools or workplaces. The majority of those who menstruate are women, who already on average earn less than men in what is known as the gender pay gap. Kenya has become a world leader in improving menstrual hygiene access. It was the first country in the world to remove taxes on tampons in 2004 and now provides free pads to schools in low-income communities.

Queer feminism

In many societies around the world, gender roles and sexual identities are highly fluid and not tied to purported biological sex. A queer feminist perspective centres on the understanding that gender is constructed from birth as a way of acting, talking and thinking. In fact, there are numerous alternative forms of gender expression around the world outside of the gender binary of being a 'woman' or a 'man'. People's sexual orientation – whom they feel attracted to and want to have romantic relationships with – is also diverse. Recognizing different possibilities of experiencing the world pushes back against heteronormative ideas that relations should be between people of opposite sex. Cross-cultural examples also show that the rigid gender binary model is not universal or even needed. Queer feminists show that, in reality, the division of society into 'male' and 'female' oppresses women and men and those who do not fit into strict gender roles. But still, people have battled extreme discrimination in order to live and love as they choose.

A non-contemporary drawing of King Nzinga Mbande.

We are living in a world for which old forms of activism are not enough and today's activism is about creating coalitions between communities.
– Angela Davis

A female king

King Nzinga Mbande (1583–1663) reigned over the Matamba and Ndongo kingdoms in modern-day Angola. Nzinga fought against the encroachment of the Portuguese colonial empire and the rapidly expanding slave trade in a reign that lasted 37 years. Nzinga ruled using the title of N*golaå* or 'king', dressed in full male clothing and with a harem of effeminate young men and female wives. Although Nzinga was in a privileged position to exert a flexible queer identity based on desire and love, their female husbandry shows the fluidity of gender and sexuality in pre-colonial Africa.

Queer – gender and sexual non-conformism.

Gender – socially constructed aspects of being male or female. These social roles are context-specific and change according to circumstances and across generations.

In Nepal, Pakistan, Bangladesh and India, hijra have been legally recognized as a 'third gender'.

Non-binary expression in Hindu society

For thousands of years Hindu society has revered non-binary gender expression. Hindu holy texts, including the *Mahabharata* and the *Ramayana*, depict gods transforming into third genders. Although there are many alternative-gender traditions in South Asia, the most common are *hijras*. Typically, *hijras* are born biologically male or intersex, but act and dress in hyper-feminine ways. Hijras often perform important societal functions. Many held important positions in royal courts, particularly during Mughal-era India from the 16th to the 19th centuries. To this day, *hijra* are considered good luck and are invited to bless births and weddings. However, many *hijras* also experience extreme discrimination, much of which was exacerbated under British colonial rule (1858–1947) when anti-*hijra* laws were enacted. Since that time, leaders and organizers have come together to protest at discriminatory policies against *hijra*. Yet many *hijras* still live on the social fringes, supporting themselves by begging and sex work, and are targets of hate crimes.

The Bugis

The Bugis are the largest ethnic group in South Sulawesi in Indonesia. Now, most Bugis are Muslim, but pre-Islamic Bugis worldview sees gender on a spectrum. Unlike the gender binary, five genders are recognized in Bugis society. Gender is highly fluid and even attempting to define Bugis conceptions of gender through Western language is limiting, but they are best understood as: *makkunrai* ('female women'), *oroané* ('male men'), *calalai* ('female men'), *calabai* ('male women') and *bissu* ('transgender or intersex priests'). In Bugis society, the *bissu* are part of an ancient tradition, seen as intermediaries between people and gods. For centuries, *bissu* served as spiritual advisers and healers in the royal courts in South Sulawesi. However, after independence in 1949, *bissu* experienced extreme persecution, with many said to be of 'deviant' sexuality and being killed. Since that time, *bissu* have been struggling to be publicly accepted again.

In South Sulawesi, bissu *non-gender binary priests belong to a tradition predating the arrival of Islam in Indonesia in the 13th century.*

Judith Butler

The American sociologist and gender theorist Judith Butler (b. 1956) popularized a performative theory of gender, which is foundational to queer feminist theory. Butler reinterprets Simone de Beauvoir's famous statement from *The Second Sex* (1949) that 'one is not born a woman but becomes one' to show how society inscribes our gender and sexuality on our physical bodies. In *Gender Trouble* (1990), Butler argues that gender *and* sex are not something fixed or anatomical facts. We are 'constructed' in ways that we do not choose from the moment of birth. In fact, societies exhibit tremendous variability in the practices and meanings that are associated with being female or a male. This shows us that gender is culturally constructed. It is also something that we often perform unconsciously, and which we do not have a completely free choice about. We act and speak and talk and walk in ways that consolidate an impression of being a man or being a woman.

Queer feminist theory challenges the concept of 'essentialism' or the idea that there is something innate to being a 'woman' or a 'man'. Queer feminists question why we categorize and assign people roles based on purported physical characteristics. Oftentimes, the principal characteristics of an individual's biological sex do not fit into two neatly distinct categories of male and female. In fact, being born with ambiguous genitals, anatomy or chromosomes – often referred to as intersex – is actually very common. It is estimated that one in 1,500 births are atypical in terms of genitalia, and more than that when it comes to more subtle sex-anatomy variations. Even when a person's biological sex is identified according to binary lines, it is unforeseeable what gender role they may play in a particular culture.

Although roles of 'male' and 'female' have cultural variations, men have come to occupy dominant social orders in many societies at the expense of women and those outside of the gender binary. In general, women still have less autonomy and access to power, and are paid less. At the same time, men can also experience oppression in some societies: such as a strict adherence to masculine gender roles, lack of equal rights to parenthood and a duty to be household economic 'providers' through work.

Judith Butler.

Sylvia Rivera

Sylvia Rivera (1951–2002) was a Latina transgender rights and gay liberation activist. Together with Marsha P. Johnson, Rivera co-founded the Street Transvestite Action Revolutionaries (STAR), which provided housing and support to homeless LGBTQ+ youth. Rivera and other trans activists highlight the need for feminism to be more inclusive of those who do not fit the mainstream. Nor, they argue, is there anything innate to being a man or a woman – a biological essentialist view that some feminists promote.

Sylvia Rivera.

Marsha P Johnson.

Marsha P. Johnson
The American gay liberation activist and drag queen Marsha P. Johnson (1945–92) was a key advocate for gay rights and a prominent figure in the Stonewall Uprising of 1969.

The fight for gay rights

From the poetry of same-sex desire written by Sappho in ancient Greece in the seventh century BCE to the gender fluidity of Native American 'Two-Spirits' to the 'female husbands' of Kenya, alternatives to Western male/female heterosexual binaries have thrived across millennia around the world. But the push for gay rights has not been without its struggles. For lesbian and gay movements, goals have included challenging dominant stereotypes of 'femininity' and 'masculinity' and heteronormative ideas of the family, along with dealing with homophobic attacks against gay couples and individuals. Politically, activists have pushed for equal-rights legislation and protection from harm and discrimination.

Because of the focus on male sexuality through the greater part of social history, lesbian partnerships are often obscured. In some cases, female relationships are not as readily accepted or are heavily sexualized for male fantasies. In recent years, activists have done much to advance acceptance of same-sex relations between women.

THE STONEWALL UPRISING

The uprising was a watershed moment for the 20th-century gay liberation movement, not just in the USA but also around the world. The violent police raid of the Stonewall Inn, a gay bar in Greenwich Village in New York City, on 28 June 1969 sparked a series of demonstrations by residents who demanded the right to live openly without fear of arrest. After Stonewall, gay liberation movements and Pride marches began to rise up worldwide to fight for equality.

The first gay pride marches took place in Chicago, Los Angeles, New York and San Francisco in 1970, a year after the Stonewall Uprising, to mark the anniversary. Since then, LGBTQ+ Pride events are held annually in June around the world, such as the Tokyo Rainbow Pride March.

Same-sex partnerships have been given important visibility in recent years, advancing gay civil rights protection in a context of extreme discrimination. However, critical gender studies scholars point out that being LGBTQ+ is not a monolithic or universal identity. The gay rights discourse can be helpful in appealing to international legal frameworks and universal notions of rights, but it can also gloss over the diversity of expressions of human sexuality and gender identity around the world.

Audre Lorde

Audre Lorde (1934–92) was a self-described 'Black, lesbian, mother, warrior, poet' who focused her work on confronting injustices of racism, sexism, classism and homophobia. Lorde's poetry and spoken word calls for an intersectional understanding of the complexity of women's experiences. In both her activism and published work, she advanced a coalitional politics that organizes across marginalized groups based on shared, but differing, experiences of oppression, such as those that arise through race, gender, sexual orientation, class, age and ability.

Alexya Salvador

Alexya Salvador (b. 1980) is a Brazilian educator and the first transgender pastor in Latin America. Salvador focuses her advocacy on addressing the violent climate against trans people in Brazil, which has the world's highest rate of anti-trans homicides.

MUJERES CREANDO

The Bolivian feminist collective Mujeres Creando or 'Women Creating' was started by Julieta Paredes, María Galindo and Mónica Mendoza in 1992 in La Paz, Bolivia. It emerged at a time in Bolivia when Spanish-descended white male elites dominated Bolivian politics. Since colonial times, class and ethnicity have profoundly divided Bolivia. Spanish conquistadores overthrew the Incan empire in the 16th century, subjecting indigenous people to extreme exploitation in the forced mining for silver. Even after independence in 1847, indigenous people and Western-oriented middle and upper classes remained deeply polarized. During the 1990s, successive political administrations put through a series of policies that privatized state-owned enterprises, resulting in a loss of public services in transportation and increasing prices for essential commodities such as water. Many of these policies benefited Bolivian elites at the expense of low-income and majority indigenous people.

Two of the founders are prominent lesbian activists in Bolivia, including María Galindo, who takes artistic practice out of the elite gallery into public spaces to provoke conversations about sexism, structural discrimination against those who are LGBTQ+, and continued Western domination.

In 2002, *Mujeres Creando gained national attention for supporting a group called Deudora ('debtor'), comprised of poor women from the barrios protesting against the crippling rates of interest on their microcredit loans. One action they took was to provide paint for the Deudora women to dip their feet into and leave their footprints on the wall, to symbolize their long journey to the capital. After months of protest and a high-profile occupation of the Bolivian Banking Supervisory Agency, they were able to convene a meeting of the banking and financial associations and Deudora, leading to those whose houses were being auctioned off having their debts excused.*

Women in Bolivia navigate a challenging landscape, with a high prevalence of domestic violence, maternal mortality and female illiteracy among indigenous communities. Extreme machismo in popular advertising cements stereotypes of women as passive, sexual objects, and of heterosexual relationships as the norm. Mujeres Creando focuses on realizing a coalitional politics of organizing with other groups based on shared – but also different – experiences of oppression. It is made up of LGBTQ+ individuals and women of all skin colours, ethnic backgrounds, ages and socio-economic positions.

Mujeres Creando run cultural centres in La Paz and Santa Cruz, publish a biweekly paper and books, run a radio programme and take part in public debates, but are best known for their creative direct actions. Since its inception, the founders have used graffiti as a means of social participation and resistance, with slogans across buildings in Bolivia's capital city, La Paz, reading 'For her the blame, for him the apology', 'You cannot decolonize without depatriarchalizing', and 'Eva will not come out of Evo's rib', in reference to then president, Evo Morales.

Chapter
6 WOMEN AND CULTURE

Since the earliest times, women have been trailblazers in fashion, music, film, literature, sports and the arts. At times combating discrimination to achieve recognition, they have also faced extreme pressures to conform to gender normative ideals. Many inspirational female, transgender and non-gender binary creatives have used their artistic practices to make powerful commentary on repressive societal norms.

Members of The Spirit of Angela perform traditional African dances at the Festival of Nations in St Louis, Missouri, USA on 26 August 2018.

The politics of fashion

Clothing is an important form of social expression for many people around the world. In some cases, it can be a tool of empowerment and a way to challenge conformity, as well as a means of collective identity. Fashion designers, such as the British fashion icon and activist Dame Vivienne Westwood (b. 1941), have also used fashion as a platform to protest on global issues. Westwood is a pioneer in sustainable fashion who, along with other luxury fashion designers such as Stella McCartney (b. 1971), campaigns against the environmental and human impacts of the fashion industry.

The fashion industry contributes enormously to the climate and ecological emergency experienced around the world. It is estimated that textile production, such as of cotton and synthetics like polyester, contributes around 38 per cent of annual greenhouse gas emissions. Beyond the production of raw materials, the manufacturing, transportation, packaging and selling of garments entails a heavy carbon footprint. The problem is then exacerbated by the trend of 'fast fashion',

Vivienne Westwood and other Climate Revolution supporters wearing T-shirts designed by Westwood.

whereby people buy excessive amounts of clothing, only wear them a few times, rarely repair their garments and then throw them away without recycling them. To counter this, some fashion designers have united to advance a sustainable approach to fashion, including using new sustainable materials and technology, recycled textiles, solar panels and LEDs for energy in production, and recyclable materials for packaging. Under the auspices of UN Climate Change, a group of leading fashion brands and NGOs created the Fashion Industry Charter for Climate Action in 2018 to move the textile, clothing and fashion industry towards net-zero greenhouse gas emissions by 2050.

As part of their commitments, companies are also focusing not just on the ecological environment but also on the environment for their employees. Much of the textile production of garments is carried out in the Global South, where employers have evaded health and safety standards and paid workers minimal wages. An equitable fashion industry is one in which garment workers have more control over the production process – including through co-operative ownership – and can earn a decent wage with dignity. This chapter looks at the ways in which women have advanced transformative change past and present through cultural practices, whether it be through fashion, the creative arts or sports.

The gender politics of fashion

The idea of dress being gendered is a recent invention. The belief systems that societies attach to clothing vary tremendously across time and place. Different cultures around the world adhere to different ways of dressing, some of which is gender neutral and not split along gender lines. Across millennia, tunics, robes, togas, kimonos, sarongs, make-up and even high heels have been worn by people of all gender orientations.

In some cultures, clothing has become part of the social practices of becoming gendered. For instance, little girls are encouraged to wear pink frilly dresses and little boys, blue trousered outfits. In Western European countries, the development of a gender binary in

COLONIAL CONFORMITY

Both genders traditionally wear animal hide and fur trousers among the Inuit of Alaska, Arctic Canada and Greenland. With the extremities of cold, dresses and skirts would be impractical. European missionary influence led to the imposition of Western women's attire, such as long skirts or dresses. These forms of governance over people's clothing and lives were common in many colonial contexts.

A series of fashionable
couples pictured in the
17th, 18th and early 19th
centuries shows the radical
difference between men's
and women's dress that
had become commonplace.

clothing kick-started in the 19th century. Separations grew between 'serious' and 'athletic' menswear and 'frivolous' female dress. Dressing norms gradually became aggressively enforced in some schools, as well as in religious and professional settings. In response, people of all genders, including those who are non-binary, have used clothing as a way of subverting gender stereotypes.

The corset debate: mark of feminine fragility and entrapment or sexual agency and social mobility?

In Western countries, the corset was embedded deeply within social constructions of gender and sexuality. Hugely popular from the 1700s onwards, the intricate structure of bone and steel moulded women's – and sometimes men's – bodies into an hourglass shape. This item of dress connected to the idealization of women's bodies, emphasizing a sexualized and fecund female physique. Wearing corsets has been heavily criticized, especially by medical professionals during the era of 'tightlacing', when women were encouraged to wear tightly laced corsets to cosmetically modify their figures. Second-wave feminists charged that the corset pandered to masculine ideals of femininity, restricting women's movements, rendering them unfit for work, and sexualizing their bodies for the male gaze. But others, particularly later feminists focusing on bodily choice, argue that the style of dress also enabled women to experiment with their own sexuality. During the Middle Ages in Europe, the body was said to be sinful, so women wore loose-fitting dresses that covered their bodies. For some, corsetry was a means of empowerment that enabled women to play with sexual subjectivities. The corset also indicated status and privilege and could be worn by women of all classes to their social advantage.

The extreme corseted appearance was a feature of women's fashion for centuries but reached its most extreme form during the later years of the 19th century.

The practice of binding the feet of young girls in China was a status symbol and mark of feminine beauty, but one that limited women's mobility and resulted in agonizing disabilities. It might seem shocking to Westerners, but is foot binding really any different to corset wearing? Ultimately, it comes down to a question of choice and the agency of the wearer.

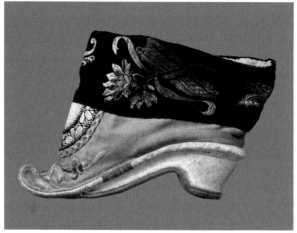

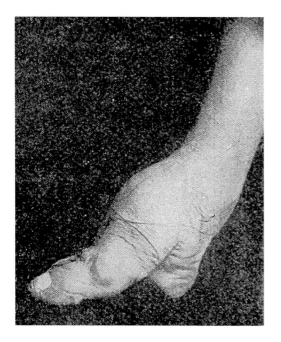

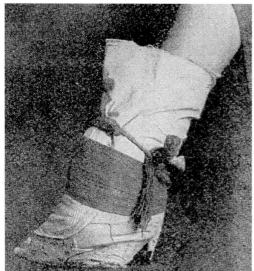

THE MODERN CORSET

In the 1980s, fashion designers manipulated the restrictive corset as a form of post-second-wave feminist empowerment. The pop icon Madonna famously wore a pink satin Jean Paul Gaultier corset with conical-stitched breasts on her 1990 Blond Ambition tour. Rather than hidden as a shaping underlayer, the corset was boldly and ironically sported as outerwear. Some argued that this symbolized a defiance of patriarchal control. For others, it reflects a cultural fixation with an artificial silhouette, achieved through extreme means.

Qiu Jin

Qiu Jin (1875–1907) was a Chinese feminist, organizer and writer, considered a feminist revolutionary martyr in China. One of her poems starts with the lines, 'Don't tell me women / are not the stuff of heroes.' Jin spoke out about foot binding, a well-established practice at the time. She promoted anti-foot-binding societies and publicly voiced the need for women's involvement in education, commerce and direct political action. She co-founded a radical women's journal, *China Women's News*, and headed a school focused on training revolutionaries against the ruling Qing dynasty. Jin was executed for her revolutionary activities at the age of 31.

Statue of Qiu Jin.

Gender-fluid fashion

In Western cultures, gender has been defined as two poles of masculine and feminine, when in reality it is a spectrum. Now, fashion designers are popularizing gender-fluid fashion, pushing back on segregated ideas of womenswear and menswear that are divided down gender lines. That fashion designers are supporting the visibility of gender fluidity is important. However, gender-fluid dressing is very much a subjective act that is better understood as a mentality of free choice.

Gladys Bentley

Gladys Bentley (1907–60) was an American blues singer and pianist during the Harlem Renaissance. She famously wore a tailcoat and top hat in her performances. Owing to her gender nonconformity as a child, she was heavily ostracized by her family and peers, which led to her being labelled as 'socially maladjusted' by psychiatrists. As a result, she left home at a young age and became successful as an entertainer in New York City. Throughout her life, she exerted a powerful Black female masculinity that still inspires LGBTQ+ and African American communities to this day.

Gladys Bentley resplendent in white tie.

CHALLENGING CONFORMITY
THROUGH FASHION: FRIDA KAHLO

A photo of Frida Kahlo showing her typically vivid dress.

The Mexican painter Frida Kahlo (1907–54) used art, clothing and her body as a direct act of political resistance and rejection of Western feminist ideals. Despite growing up in a time of gender inequality, Kahlo did not conform to societal pressures. During an era when women were legally restricted in their clothing choice in some regions of the world, Kahlo boldly wore a suit in family portraits. She also refused to change her features, such as her mono-brow and faint moustache. Instead, she exaggerated her features even more in her self-portraits, and simultaneously embraced brightly coloured traditional dress from Mexico's Isthmus of Tehuantepec – a region famous for its powerful matriarchal organization.

Kahlo's paintings focused on female concerns, including abortion, miscarriage and breastfeeding: subjects that were considered taboo at the time and rarely spoken of in public. Kahlo was openly bisexual and had relationships with women and men, including the iconic French entertainer and civil rights activist Josephine Baker.

A major factor in Kahlo's life was that she suffered from multiple disabilities, including spinal bifida, a congenital condition that affected her spinal development, which was heightened from contracting polio as a young child. The polio virus damaged her right leg and foot, which was ultimately amputated in 1953. At the age of 18, she was in a severe bus accident, in which she broke her collarbone, spinal column and right foot. As a result, she had to rely on adaptive footwear, medical corsets and prosthetic devices to physically support her. Kahlo painted and decorated her prosthetic leg and corsets, gaining control and power over her body and making a challenging impairment beautiful. She has thus been an inspirational icon for those living with disabilities and for feminism at large in her defiance against conformity.

Kahlo designed her prosthetic leg to have a glamorous bright-red lace-up wedge boot with Chinese silk embroidery. She herself said that this was a way of taking possession of a functional and ugly implement and making it beautiful for her own enjoyment.

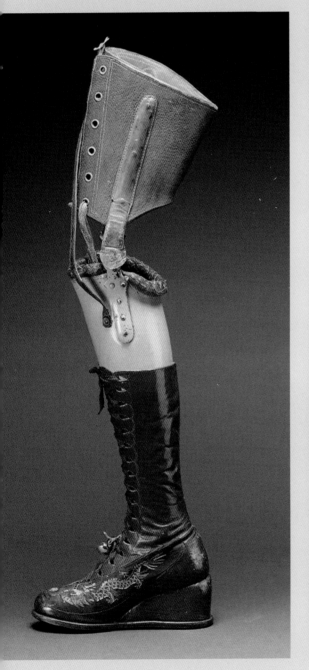

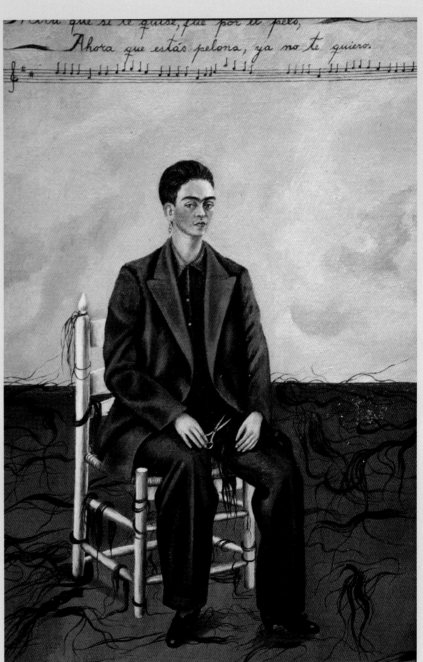

Frida Kahlo, Self-Portrait with Cropped Hair (1940).

Marlene Dietrich

The German Hollywood actress Marlene Dietrich (1901–92) pushed the boundaries of fashion's gender constructs. She often wore tuxedos and trousers at a time when this was considered scandalous. Rumours circulated that Dietrich was arrested in Paris owing to a French law that banned women from wearing trousers – a law that was not formally repealed until 2013! Dietrich was influential for generations of women, giving many the confidence and power of wearing suits.

Billy Porter

The American actor, singer and author Billy Porter (b. 1969) uses fashion to make political statements, including around gender conventions and the rules placed on individuals in life. Porter famously wore a Christian Siriano tuxedo gown at the 2019 Oscars as a challenge to conventional gender-conforming fashion. Younger artists are also shaping the future of queer representation through fashion and other cultural media, as well as breaking the boundaries of binary fashion.

Marlene Dietrich in her beloved trouser suits.

Billy Porter at the Oscars in a skirted version of black tie.

In Madagascar, men and women both wear a lamba, which is a colourful textile wrapped around the body and worn on traditional ceremonial occasions.

Women and the arts

Gender bias is far less overt today, although women artists continue to face hurdles and under-representation in museums, galleries and public fora. This neglect is certainly not down to a dearth of female artists, but rather a longstanding bias towards male dominance in the arts. Women artists comprise only 3–5 per cent of major art museum collections in Europe and the USA. Female characters in films still receive roughly half of the dialogue and screen time of their male counterparts. While there are more women in arts management, it is men who more commonly hold upper-management positions and earn higher salaries. Efforts to push back on these gender disparities are giving more visibility to the creative energies of women around the world.

Louise Bourgeois

The French artist Louise Bourgeois (1911–2010) remains a prominent figure of contemporary art, known for her large-scale sculptures and installations. Many of her later works use the spider to symbolize the mother figure, as both predator and protector. For Bourgeois, the spider was partly a reference to her own mother, who worked in tapestry restoration, and to herself. She often used hard materials, such as in her spider series, to disrupt the stereotypical associations of softness with femininity.

Maman *or 'Mom'* (1999).

Bourgeois pushed back on some of her contemporary surrealist male artists, who made women the object of their work, whereas she focused on making women the subject. Despite this, she was not keen to be labelled as a feminist artist, not wanting to have her art analysed only through feminist themes. Yet Bourgeois's prominence in a male-dominated art world has supported the recognition of women's artistic talents.

Betye Saar

Betye Saar (b. 1926) is an African American artist who uses the medium of assemblage – drawing together found and self-made objects and mixed media – to make powerful comments against stereotypes and myths of race and femininity. Saar was a crucial part of the Black Arts Movement in the 1970s, along with poets and writers like Audre Lorde, Maya Angelou, Ntozake Shange and Nikki Giovanni, who looked to find new ways of presenting the Black experience. Saar's own experiences of marginalization from the white feminist arts movement prompted her to promote a Black female consciousness. She pushed back on ideas of the 'feminine aesthetic' as something determined by white feminists. In artworks such as *The Liberation of Aunt Jemima* (1972), she incorporated racist imagery of Black women ('Aunt Jemima' was a racist stereotype of Black women domestic workers) as a way of reclaiming them into symbols of empowerment. Saar's exploration of the Black female body also made powerful social commentary on the visual representation of African American women, from a time when Black women's bodies were hypersexualized or rendered invisible and used to further racist ideology.

Many of Saar's artworks feature washboards as a symbol of Black women's labour. She made visible an object that signalled oppression and violence, bringing it centre stage from the margins and transforming it into something revolutionary. Some of Saar's washboards hold references to the civil rights movement, Black activism and police brutality. By recycling objects, Saar shows how entrenched racism is in the USA in ways that are structurally embedded. But with each generation, Saar argues that the world is becoming progressively cleaner.

We Was Mostly 'Bout Survival (1997) *depicts a Black female domestic worker on a washboard, surrounded by the phrases 'national racism', 'liberate Aunt Jemima' and 'We was mostly 'bout survival'. The work makes powerful commentary on oppression and the division of labour based on race and gender, while also calling out racist stereotypes through imagery and text.*

Ingrid Pollard

Later artists like the British-Guyanese photographer Ingrid Pollard (b. 1953) have explored themes surrounding gender and race. Pollard uses portraiture and landscape photography to think through social constructs around Britishness and racial difference. Her series *Pastoral Interlude* is a series of portraits of Black women and men in English countryside scenes to challenge racial stereotypes of rural England that invariably imagine Black people in urban settings.

Yayoi Kusama

Yayoi Kusama (b. 1929) is a Japanese artist known for her distinctive use of polka dots in her paintings, sculptures, performances and installations. Kusama came to public attention as part of the 1960s avant-garde, when she organized a series of art 'happenings' in New York City, covering the bodies of naked women and men with her signature polka dots. Kusama's work championed sexual liberation, using the body as a canvas, while making critical political commentaries against the Vietnam War, capitalism and the dominance of white men in art museums' collection holdings. In *Walking Piece* (1966), Kusama walked through the streets of New York City in a Japanese kimono with a black umbrella as a parasol, decorated with fake flowers and crying unreservedly. Through her performance, she emphasized the stereotypes that Asian women face as a commentary on her outsider status owing to her ethnicity and gender. Kusama herself has struggled with mental health challenges. She has voluntarily lived at a psychiatric institute in Tokyo since 1977. Her famous immersive 'infinity mirror rooms' of coloured lights and polka dots are powerful expressions of her inner world, which she describes as filled with hallucinations and psychological distress.

ABOVE: *Ingrid Pollard.*

LEFT: *Yayoi Kusama.*

Tracey Emin

Tracey Emin (b. 1963) is a British artist who uses personal narratives and objects to explore ideas of gender and femininity. Many of her artworks incorporate objects from her life and home, in which she blurs artistic and autobiographical practice. She was at the forefront of the Young British Artists scene in the 1990s, a group known for their shock tactics who achieved substantial media coverage. In her work, Emin denounces social restrictions, instead pushing back on gender-specific stereotypes surrounding appropriateness and femininity. Emin is best known for her *My Bed* (1998), which was a shortlisted work for the Turner Prize. The piece consisted of Emin's unmade bed strewn with bedroom objects such as slippers, empty alcohol bottles, cigarette packets and underwear: quite different to how women's beds have been represented in Western, largely male, artistic traditions. Emin created the work in her council flat in London after a bout of extreme depression following the end of a relationship. Other works, such as *Everyone I Have Ever Slept With 1963–1995* (1997), a tent covered with the names of her partners, challenged societal expectations of women as chaste and undisclosing of their sexuality. Many of Emin's works also revolve around questions of social class, using street language to confront intellectual art speak. Along with Fiona Rae, Emin was the first female professor at the Royal Academy of Arts since its founding in 1768.

Tracey Emin on her famously unmade bed.

Strategy (South Face/Front Face/North Face) (1994), Jenny Saville.

Jenny Saville

The British artist Jenny Saville (b. 1970) is also a seminal figure from the Young British Artist scene. In her work, she contests depictions of the idealized female body that has been historically promoted by male artists. Instead, she paints realistic representations of women. Saville has said, 'I'm not trying to teach, just make people discuss, look at how women have been made by man. What is beauty? Beauty is usually the male image of the female body. My women are beautiful in their individuality.'

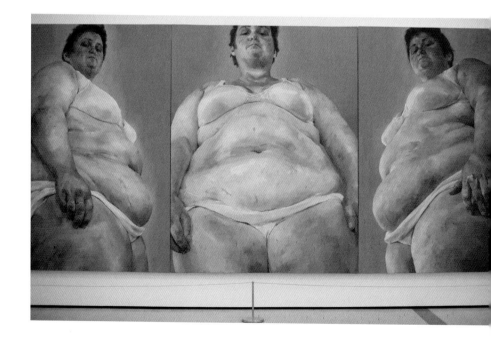

Billie Zangewa (right) and her tapestry *Soldier of Love* (2020).

Billie Zangewa

Billie Zangewa (b. 1973) is a Malawian-South African artist who creates hand-sewn silk fabrics into collage tapestries. Much of her work is autobiographical and foregrounds Black femininity, everyday domesticity and motherhood. In her silk tapestry *The Rebirth of the Black Venus* (2010), Zangewa references Botticelli's *The Birth of Venus* (1486) and the tragic experiences of Saartjie Baartman – the so-called 'Hottentot Venus' – who was a South African Khoikhoi woman exhibited as an attraction in 19th-century Europe. Both examples illustrate how Black women's bodies were objectified or made invisible through socio-normative and racist representations of ideals of feminine beauty. In her artwork, Zangewa instead depicts the Venus Pudica as a Black woman floating over the city of Johannesburg, making her into a contemporary goddess.

Meanwhile, in silk tapestries such as *Soldier of Love* (2020), Zangewa creates portraits of everyday scenes through a textile medium traditionally seen as a female craft, but which Zangewa shows to be a subtly politically subversive tool. She turns the attention to the taken-for-granted domestic labour largely of women that forms the backbone of many societies. These intimate portraits of Black women's personal lives, Zangewa argues, are still heavily marginalized.

Wendy Red Star

Wendy Red Star (b. 1981) is a Native American multimedia artist from Montana and a member of the Apsáalooke (Crow) tribe. In her work, she pushes back on romanticized representations of Native Americans to offer new understandings of American settler colonial history. She uses the title *Apsáalooke Feminist* to highlight the ironies of applying the Western term 'feminism' to the matrilineal culture of the Crow Nation, a movement that was a product of colonialism and long marginalized women of colour, while presenting feminist liberation as something exceptional to white EuroAmericans. Red Star has focused on advancing forums for Native American women's voices in contemporary art, without being integrated as an 'exotic' special division.

Wendy Red Star.

Jane Jacobs

Jane Jacobs (1916–2006) was a highly influential Canadian American urban theorist, journalist and social activist whose book *The Death and Life of Great American Cities* (1961) changed cities around the world. Jacobs argued that the earlier urban planning efforts advanced by largely white men advocated for high-rises and highways and were actively destroying urban life. She fought against corporate developers to advance a focus on community and street-level interaction, such as making streets more walkable, supporting local businesses and integrating communal green spaces. Jacobs also fought and won against highway development, in particular against New York City planners trying to build an expressway through Lower Manhattan. There are limits to Jacobs's urban philosophies. Without a commitment to affordable public housing, rent and property tax regulation, the implementation of her' blueprints has seen mass gentrification, with neighbourhoods in cities such as Portland, San Francisco, Austin and New Orleans skyrocketing in rent. Jacobs warned that urban development could increase social inequality unless underlying issues of poverty and unequal access to opportunities were addressed.

Lina Bo Bardi

Like Jacobs, the Italian-Brazilian modernist architect Lina Bo Bardi (1914–92) also placed people at the centre of design, merging ambitious architecture with the everyday. Bo Bardi's designs were used for the São Paulo Museum of Art and major theatres and cultural centres across São Paulo and Salvador. SESC Pompéia, a social and cultural centre in São Paulo, houses swimming, football, theatre, art and dance, as well as places for people to gather and enjoy each other's company, including tables for playing chess, parks and boardwalks. Bo Bardi is recognizable for her unique style, combining Italian modernism with Brazilian characteristics. She even used a technique for constructing wooden stairs adapted from the construction of ox carts! One of Bo Bardi's most iconic buildings is the 'Casa de Vidro' or 'Glass House', where she personally lived, deep in the rain forest surrounding São Paulo. The house is raised on stilts with forest views throughout the glass walls, rooting a modernist design into the local environment. Many of Bo Bardi's buildings embrace environmental interaction, with channels to allow water to cascade through during Brazil's tropical rainy seasons. In 2021, she became the first female architect to receive the Special Golden Lion for Lifetime Achievement: an honour received *in memoriam* at the Venice Biennale.

Jane Jacobs

SESC *Pompéia, designed by Lina Bo Bardi.*

Women and the silver screen

Acting stars around the world generally occupy centre stage, but women are trailblazers in front of *and* behind the silver screen. For as long as the movie industry has existed, women have been making films and advancing revolutionary techniques. So, although the Lumière brothers are often cited as the pioneers of motion pictures, with their short films from the late 1800s making them some of the world's earliest film-makers, they were not unique.

Alice Guy-Blaché

French film-maker Alice Guy-Blaché (1873–1968) was pioneering her own techniques in the groundbreaking artform at the same time as the Lumière brothers, using film to tell stories rather than as technological spectacle. She advanced now-standard technical skills such as editing, special effects and colour. She likely even invented the music video in 1905, using the new 'chronophone' technology to film singers lip-syncing to music. Throughout her career, Guy-Blaché made more than 1,000 films, from comedies to dramas to westerns. Her film *The Consequences of Feminism* (1906) imagines a world of reversed gender-stereotyped roles, where women smoke and fight while men sew and iron at home.

Guy-Blaché had a huge influence on the development of film but has largely been written out of film history in favour of her male counterparts.

Florence Lois Weber

Florence Lois Weber (1879–1939) was an American silent film actress, director, screenwriter and producer. She is known as one of the most important and prolific silent film directors. In 1916, she was the highest-paid studio director of any gender in the USA. Like Guy-Blaché, she pioneered groundbreaking cinematic techniques, such as split screen and double exposure. Many of her films used early devices for creating tension in suspenseful films, such as a shot of a telephone wire being slit with a knife. She was also a trailblazer for bringing the conversation of birth control on to film, at a time when both birth control and abortion were illegal.

The controversial Florence Lois Weber.

Other women film-makers in early Hollywood

Weber and Guy-Blaché were not alone as early pioneers of film-making. In fact, for a while, women dominated the film industry. Dorothy Arzner (1897–1979) established a long, successful career in Hollywood as a film director, launching the careers of Hollywood actresses like Katharine Hepburn and Lucille Ball. Frances Marion (1888–1973) was the highest-paid screenwriter of the 1920s and '30s, who began her film career working for Lois Weber's film production company. After being employed as a foreign correspondent during World War I, she went on to become the first writer to win two Academy Awards. Mabel Normand (1893–1930) was known as the 'mother of comedy' and directed Charlie Chaplin's first portrayal of his famous character The Tramp. The film-maker Tressie Souders (1897–1995) was the first African American woman director to direct a feature film, A *Woman's Error*, in 1922.

During the 1920s and '30s, some of Hollywood's most progressive films were made. Gender roles were challenged; there were stories of women in power, making their own choices and not conforming to alleged feminine expectations. However, conditions

Dorothy Arzner is to this day the most prolific woman studio director in American cinematic history, directing a number of features such as Christopher Strong *and* Craig's Wife *that upended traditional views of women's roles.*

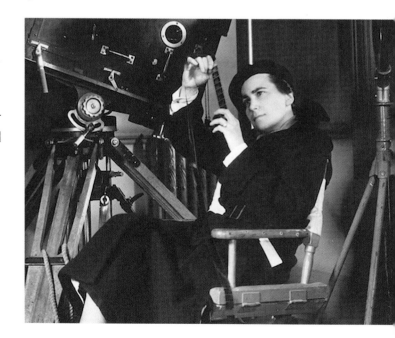

for women in Hollywood changed with the passing of the conservative Hays Code in 1934, which set moral standards for the representation of women and men in film. Instead, women became passive love interests with their bodies closely regulated. The code was also overtly racist and forbade the depiction of relationships between couples with different skin colours on screen. The Hays Code was revoked in 1968, but it had a huge effect on how women and men are portrayed in film.

THE BECHDEL TEST

This litmus test, devised by the American cartoonist Alison Bechdel (b. 1960), measures the representation of women in fiction. It is often used to figure out not just whether women appear on screen but *how* they appear. To pass the test, a film has to answer yes to three questions:

1. Are there at least two named female characters?

2. Do the women have a conversation at any point?

3. Do they talk about something other than a man?

This might seem incredibly easy, but few films pass this test! On average, 40 per cent of films fail, including some that have female leads or are directed and written by females. Other tests have since been devised to measure the inclusion of people of colour, LGBTQ+ people and those of minority religious and ethnic backgrounds.

Chinoye Chukwu.

Chinonye Chukwu

Chinonye Chukwu (b. 1985) is a Nigerian film director who has written films with powerful female leads, such as *The Dance Lesson* (2010), about a young Black girl trying to become a ballerina in a gentrifying community; *Clemency* (2019), which focused on a female prison warden coping with the challenges of her job; and *Till* (2022), a biographical film about the mother of the 14-year-old Emmett Louis Till who was lynched in 1955 by white supremacists.

Anne V. Coates.

Anne V. Coates

The British film editor Anne V. Coates (1925–2018) had an impressive 60-year career. She was known for her editorial work on the legendary epic *Lawrence of Arabia* (1962), which won her an Oscar. She also edited Oscar-winning films such as *The Elephant Man* (1980) and *Out of Sight* (1998).

Lina Wertmüller

The Italian film director Lina Wertmüller (1928–2021) was the first woman to be nominated for an Oscar, in 1977 for her film *Seven Beauties* (1975). She also wrote the screenplays for her movies, although she often faced criticism for her low representation of women. It was not until 1994 that another woman would be nominated for best director: the New Zealand director Jane Campion (b. 1954), for *The Piano* (1993).

Kathryn Bigelow

Kathryn Bigelow (b. 1951) became the first female director to win an Oscar, in 2010 for her film *The Hurt Locker* (2008). The film focuses on an American bomb squad that disables explosives in Iraq. Critics agree that Bigelow's work was excellent in portraying the human emotions and suspense of a war zone, but many also question why it took so long for a woman to win the world's top film-making award since its beginnings in 1929 – and then for a film with hyper-masculine subject matter.

THE WOMEN OF BOLLYWOOD

Bollywood refers to the Indian Hindi-language film industry centred in Mumbai (formerly Bombay). Beginning in the early 1900s, film-making exploded in India. In the 1960s, India overtook the US film industry as the largest site of film production in the world. Fatma Begum (1892–1983) is often considered Bollywood's first female director. Her first feature film, *Bulbul-e-Paristan* (1926) was a big-budget fantasy filled with special effects, from which she went on to launch her own production house.

Mira Nair (b. 1957), pictured here, is just one of a number of female directors making waves in Indian cinema. Her work challenges inaccurate depictions of India in Bollywood films. Instead, films like *Salaam Bombay!* (1988) integrate children living on the streets as actors to show their realities in film.

The Oscar-nominated director and screenwriter Deepa Mehta's (b. 1950) contributions to cinema have also been tremendous. In her film *Fire* (1996) from her Elements Trilogy, the love scene between two women resulted in violent protests in India, including the destruction of cinemas and government censorship. The last film from the Trilogy, *Water* (2005), focuses on the inequalities of class privilege and the extreme oppression of Indian women through conservative religious doctrines. Mehta was forced to change the filming location to Sri Lanka after Hindu fundamentalists destroyed the Ganges River film sets. She continues to advance critical conversations through film. *Funny Boy* (2020) is a queer coming-of-age tale that follows a wealthy gay Tamil boy in Sri Lanka during the time of an anti-Tamil pogrom known as 'Black July'. It remains illegal to be openly LGBTQ+ in Sri Lanka and the violence experienced by Tamils is still felt to this day.

Many Bollywood films still resort to stereotypes of women as passive, sexualized love interests or as ideal mothers in domestic roles. Film-makers have slowly pushed back on these representations, such as in *Gunjan Saxena: The Kargil Girl* (2020), which looks at the life of a young officer who became the first Indian female air force officer to fly in a combat zone in the Kargil War with Pakistan in the late 1990s.

Mira Nair

Deepa Mehta

Women and protest song

Music has long brought people together, fostering solidarity and providing social uplift in the face of violence and oppression. Spirituals are a powerful example of the use of music to counter the brutal denial of personhood. Sometimes called sorrow songs, spirituals were used by enslaved people in the abolition movement, including the Underground Railroad (see page 167), to give them the strength to keep going. Music is also used to publicly express dissatisfaction and advance social change. Artists across genres and styles call for reform, using their voices and platforms to challenge political oppression and systems of power.

Mona Haydar

Mona Haydar (b. 1988) is a Syrian American Muslim rapper whose work addresses the intersectional discrimination of Islamophobia, racism and sexism that Muslim women routinely face. The video to her debut hit single 'Hijabi (Wrap my Hijab)' (2017) features a cast of hijab-wearing Muslim women and Haydar, who is eight months pregnant. In the song, Haydar raps about the experiences of women who choose to wear the hijab. She questions Western interpretations of the hijab as a symbol of oppression, challenging the Orientalization of Muslim women and obsession with policing women's bodies. In her single 'Dog' (2017), she also highlights the sexism of Muslim men who purport to be spiritual leaders but misinterpret the Quran to justify the oppression of women. Haydar's music celebrates women's diversity, bringing Muslim feminist concerns to global audiences.

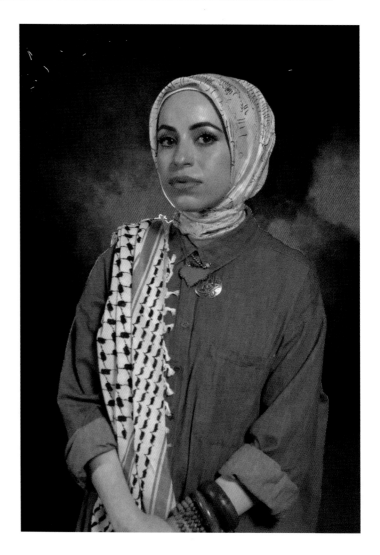

Mona Haydar, pictured in 2018.

Throat singing is an example of an informal musical practice that brings women together in solidarity. The traditional song practice of *katajjaq* began as a playful call-and-response game between two women. Facing each other, the women exchange quick rhythmic inhalations and exhalations of breath, weaving intricate patterns, until one ends up laughing or loses the beat. For many years, this powerful communal practice was banned by Western settler colonialists in an attempt to stamp out indigenous culture. The contemporary Canadian Inuq musician Tanya Tagaq (b. 1975) combines throat-singing techniques with punk, heavy metal, hip-hop and electronica. In her music, she makes important commentary on attempted indigenous erasure and the horrific numbers of missing and murdered indigenous women. In this way, Tagaq, along with new generations of Inuit women, celebrates sisterhood solidarity through *katajjaq*.

A quiet song

The song *Quiet*, written by the Los Angeles-based musician Connie K. Lim (b. 1986), known as MILCK, became the anthem of the 2017 Women's March in Washington, D.C.. She originally co-wrote the song to cope with the experience of sexual abuse as a teenager. Lim organized singers from across the USA into a #ICANTKEEPQUIET chorus as a flash mob during the Women's March. The song went viral on social media as the #MeToo movement took hold. It signified the power of women coming together to advocate around issues including domestic violence, reproductive and LGBTQ+ rights and racism.

The knitted pink caps (known as pussyhats) were worn by large numbers of women on the United States 2017 Women's March. However, they declined in popularity with many activists who argued that it excludes transgender women and gender non-binary individuals, as well as people of colour.

Oumou Sangaré and the Birds of Wassoulou

The Wasoulou region of southern Mali in West Africa is known for its powerful genre of female-led music, known as *wassolou*. The women vocalists leading this musical movement describe themselves as *konow* or 'birds'. Unlike the hereditary traditional musicians known as the *jeli* or griots, who dominate Malian musical life, *wassolou* performers occupy a different social role. They are musicians not by birth but by choice. Mande society, which encompasses a large group of peoples across West Africa, is strictly patrilineal and hierarchical. As 'birds' symbolizing freedom, wisdom, messengers, bird's-eye views of society and beautiful voices, *konow* can make powerful social commentary.

The Malian singer Oumou Sangaré is the most well-known contemporary proponent of the *wassolou* musical movement. She interweaves social and political concerns into her lyrics, singing about themes of female subjugation in marriage, polygamy and pressures on women to have children. *Wassolou* is traditionally associated with young people, incorporating the *kamalengoni* youth harp from the Wasoulou hunting tradition. The *kamalengoni* is an iconic instrument of youth rebellion in Mali, dating back to the 1960s when musicians sang about the importance of freedom in love and marriage. Sangaré's music is similarly directed towards youth to challenge social norms and advance change, including albums such as *Moussolou* ('Women') (1991), *Ko Sira* ('Marriage Today') (1993) and *Worotan* ('10 Kola Nuts': the traditional price of a bride in Mali) (1996).

A new generation of *kono* songbirds is now flying alongside Sangaré to create a neo-traditional system of *wassolou*. The Malian musician Fatoumata Diawara (b. 1982) brings in Western instrumentation and electronic sounds to sing protest songs on domestic violence, arranged marriage and education. Like Sangaré, she has collaborated with musicians from around the world, including Bobby Womack, Herbie Hancock, Damon Albarn and the Gorillaz.

As voices of the people, konow singers such as Oumou Sangaré fall outside of traditional social hierarchy and use this freedom to make powerful social commentary.

Women and sports

From football and rugby to tennis, wrestling and gymnastics, women have made indelible marks on sports for centuries. Back in 776BCE, before each ancient Olympic Games, women's athletic events were held at the Olympian stadium. These were known as the Heraean Games and were dedicated to the Greek goddess Hera.

Women also participated in the ancient ballgame of Mesoamerican civilizations known as *ulama* or *pelota*. The game was started by the Olmecs in 1500BCE on the Gulf Coast of Mexico, then popularized by the Maya then Aztecs across Central and South America. It involves players propelling a 3.6-kg (8-lb) rubber ball using their hips or forearms. Ceramic female ballplayer figurines have been found in archaeological sites, providing evidence that women also played the rubber ballgame.

A Roman mosaic from the Piazza Armerina in Sicily shows women playing sport, including a discus thrower.

THE WOMEN WRESTLERS OF SENEGAL

For centuries, women have competed in seasonal wrestling matches in Senegal in a traditional style known as *laamb*. The sport is hugely popular across the country, developing from a cultural rite of passage to celebrate harvests and mark male initiation into manhood in the southern Casamance region. Women have slowly gained entry to the sport and are now ranked among Africa's top female wrestlers.

The fight for equal pay

Women have fought for long-overdue limelight in sports. They often now generate more revenue and higher TV ratings than their male counterparts. Yet many still receive far lower pay: what is referred to as the gender pay gap. The US women's soccer team have won the last two World Cups. Players like Megan Rapinoe have become world leaders in the push for gender equity and LGBTQ inclusion. In 2022, the soccer team reached a landmark agreement with the US Soccer governing body over their struggle for equal pay. US Soccer also committed to establishing a fund to support the sport for women at large.

By contrast, tennis has one of the lowest gender pay gaps in sports. American legends like Serena Williams (b. 1981) and Venus Williams (b. 1980) now receive the same prize money in tennis Grand Slam tournaments as men. Even so, men earn more than women across the board.

The activism of sportspeople like the 39-time Grand Slam winner Billie Jean King (b. 1943) pushed the movement for gender equity in tennis. Even after King won her first Wimbledon in 1966, becoming the women's world No 1 player, she was still working as a playground instructor to pay her bills. As well as far lower pay, women had fewer competitive tournament opportunities. Tired of this, King and eight other women's professional tennis players launched their own all-female tournament. The 'Original 9' signed $1 contracts to compete in a series of matches: publicizing their protest in this famous photo in which they held up $1 bills. King also engaged in high-profile

The triumphant US soccer team celebrate after winning the 2019 FIFA Women's World Cup against the Netherlands.

The world-beating Williams sisters.

advocacy, including staging a barricade in a hotel in London! In 1973, she founded the Women's Tennis Association (WTA), which still exists, to promote women's tennis and equal pay.

Everyone thinks women should be thrilled when we get crumbs, and I want women to have the cake, the icing, and the cherry on top too.
– Billie Jean King, 1970

Billie Jean King (back row, second from left) and the other members of the 'Original 9' women tennis players.

THE SPEED SISTERS

The Speed Sisters were the first all-female car-racing team in the Middle East. Founded in 2010, the team of Palestinian women compete in autocross car races across the West Bank. Motor sports remains male dominated with cultural associations that emphasize the link between cars and masculinity, and women as peripheral participants. This is not due to a lack of skill but because there has been little willingness to support women's involvement in the sport. In this macho world, there are only a few female engineers, test drivers and presenters, and on the track, it is almost entirely men. For decades, the professional presence of women on racing tracks was most visibly as 'grid girls': hostesses in tight-fitting dresses who stand in front of cars before Grand Prix races. Following accumulated pressure, Formula 1 banned the practice of grid girls in 2018.

The Speed Sisters have tackled these challenges head-on, shattering gender stereotypes through their racing prowess. Racing is an expensive sport and they have to scramble together funds through families and friends. Some of the team are mechanics and fix their own cars, as well as those of male racers. What's more, not only must the Speed Sisters navigate patriarchal norms, but they also face the socio-economic and political struggles of racing and living in occupied Palestine. There are no official racetracks in the West Bank so the Speed Sisters and other racing teams often practise on land beside Israeli military compounds. They have been shot at and tear-gassed during their practices. Nevertheless, the fast and furious female racers continue to tear up tracks across the West Bank.

Transgender athletes

Transgender athletes are often under scrutiny from the media and sports governing bodies. The South African runner and Olympic champion Caster Semenya (b. 1991), for instance, is an intersex woman who was assigned female at birth and identifies as a woman. Because of her running prowess and physical appearance, her cisgender competitors filed charges against her, claiming that she must be a man and should not race against other women. The International Association of Athletics Federations (IAAF) therefore made Semenya undergo humiliating gender testing in order to continue competing against other women internationally. The gender test suggested that Semenya does not fit biologically into male or female categories – either because of chromosomal variations or atypical reproductive organs. Eventually, Semenya was allowed to run again, winning gold in the women's 800m in the 2012 and 2016 Olympics.

In 2018, however, the IAAF announced a new 'differences of sex development rule'. It requires runners competing in the 400m, 800m and 1500m races with naturally elevated testosterone levels to take medication to lower it or to have surgery. Many athletes have concerns about taking hormone suppressants, which can reduce their natural muscle mass. Intimate practices of body policing and evaluation, such as those Semenya was pushed to undergo, are also highly invasive and harmful to people's mental health. Who gets to decide what the standard of 'femaleness' is? And how is this decided?

Semenya is not the only athlete to be impacted by this decision. Athletes with a blend of male and female anatomical characteristics are common in sports. In 2021, Semenya lodged an appeal with the European Court of Human Rights to challenge the restriction. She, and athletes such as the Indian sprinter Dutee Chand (b. 1996), have become inspirational to gender campaigners around the world.

POLICING THE BODY IN SPORTS

The debate over transgender athletes connects to long histories of sexist debates surrounding sports as 'masculinizing' women. Consider the labelling of athletic girls as 'tomboys', sportswomen as 'butch', or boys as 'sissy' if they did not participate in so-called masculine sports.

THE IRON LADIES

The Iron Ladies are a men's volleyball team in Thailand made up of *kathoey* (third gender), trans and gay athletes. The players experienced rejection from top teams so chose to form their own side. In 1996, the Iron Ladies won the Thai national championship, but were not allowed to join the country's national volleyball team because of their 'cosmetics and women's clothes'. LGBTQ+ rights in Thailand are improving, but there are still hardly any anti-discrimination laws on the basis of sexual orientation.

Women and literature

We are not long past the time when female authors published their work under male or gender-neutral pen names. For many women writers, using a male nom de plume was the only way to publish their work in a male-dominated genre or reach a substantial audience. As was the case with many female European writers in the Victorian era, the Brontë sisters – authors of classics such as *Jane Eyre* (1847), *Emma* (1860), *Agnes Grey* (1847) and *Wuthering Heights* (1848) – published their work under pseudonyms. Charlotte was Currer, Anne was Acton, Emily was Ellis, and all took the surname of Bell. Charlotte Brontë later reflected: 'We did not like to declare ourselves women, because – without at that time suspecting that our mode of writing and thinking was not what is called "feminine" – we had a vague impression that authoresses are liable to be looked on with prejudice.'

The landmark novel *Middlemarch* (1871/72), often upheld as the greatest novel ever written for its intricately woven analysis of English provincial life, was also written by Mary Ann Evans (1819–80) under the male pen name George Eliot. Like the Brontë sisters, Evans wanted to escape the stereotype of women's writing as light-hearted romances and avoid not being taken seriously. *Middlemarch* was a literary masterpiece and highlighted crucial issues, including the status of women, education, the nature of marriage and political reform.

Charlotte, Emily and Anne Brontë, painted by their brother Branwell, who erased his own image from the picture.

Louisa May Alcott, *photographed* c.1870.

The great American novelist Louisa May Alcott (1832–88) is best known for her coming-of-age novel *Little Women* (1868). Focusing on the lives of the March sisters – Meg, Jo, Beth and Amy – the novel was acclaimed for its in-depth examination of women's lives. Although the novel and its sequels revolve around themes of marriage and domesticity, Alcott's work examines how powerful characters such as Jo battle sexist standards to become writers themselves. Alcott herself often used pen names earlier in her career because of the scandalous nature of some of her work. She wrote what she called 'blood and thunder tales' – dramatic short thrillers for adults – under the pen name A.M. Barnard, much like her character Jo March, to support her parents, who suffered from financial difficulties. Alcott was a noted abolitionist and feminist. Her father, Bronson Alcott, founded an abolitionist society and her childhood home in Concord, Massachusetts was a stop on the Underground Railroad for African Americans escaping slavery. She was the first woman to register to vote in Concord in 1879 and famously wrote, 'I'd rather be a free spinster and paddle my own canoe.'

Even in recent years, some female writers have made efforts to avoid gender bias in the reception of their work. The great American science-fiction writer Alice Norton (1912–2005) used the name Andre

THE EARLIEST AUTHOR

A *carved relief, said to be of Endheduanna.*

The Sumerian poet Enheduanna (b. 2285BCE) is considered the world's first known author. She was a high priestess of the moon deity Nanna-Suen at his temple in modern-day Iraq. Her poetry and temple hymns were popular throughout the ancient world, inspiring prayers in the Hebrew Bible and Homeric hymns of ancient Greece. Her works were written in the ancient style of cuneiform using clay tablets. Many of her poems contain autobiographical elements, such as dealing with the creative process and challenges to her political position. Her descriptions of planetary movements are also often cited as early scientific observations. There is even a crater on Mercury named after Enheduanna! In 1927, the British archeologist Charles Leonard Woolley discovered the white calcite 'disk of Enheduanna', which depicts her at work.

Norton after her publishers recommended that it would increase her marketability for male sci-fi readership. Norton was in fact the first woman to be Gandalf Grand Master of Fantasy, a SFWA Grand Master, and to be inducted into the Science Fiction and Fantasy Hall of Fame. The acclaimed British crime author P.D. James, who created the Adam Dalgliesh Mysteries, was Phyllis James (1920–2014). Even in the massively successful recent Harry Potter series, Joanne Rowling's (b. 1965) abbreviated pen name of J.K. Rowling was a deliberate recommendation from her publisher to appeal to a young male readership who might otherwise reject books written by women.

The activist poet: Anna Andreyevna Akhmatova (1889–1966)

Akhmatova was a towering figure of Russian poetry, who emerged as a distinct poetic voice prior to the Russian Revolution in the reign of Tsar Nicholas II. During the years of Stalinist terror, she chronicled the violence of the regime, becoming a beacon for a generation of dissident poets. She and her fellow Russian activist artists would read their poetry in crowded cafes, perform experimental theatre and dance, and produce powerful artworks. Her work was strongly condemned and censored by the authorities, but she chose to remain in the Soviet Union to document the traumatic events taking place around her, writing that 'there is no power more threatening and terrible than the prophetic word of the poet'.

Alice Norton wrote hundreds of novels and short stories using the pen name Andre Norton.

A painting of Anna Andreyevna Akhmatova.

Her poem cycle *Requiem* focuses directly on people's suffering under Stalinism, and especially that of women. Akhmatova ran extreme risks in writing down her poetry so she and her friends would memorize it. It was not until after Stalin's death in 1953 that her poetry was published in full. Following Akhmatova, feminist writing became more visible in Russia across the 1990s and 2000s, with a new generation of writers expressing frustrations at the government and raising topics once seen as taboo.

The Modernist Trailblazer: Virginia Woolf (1882–1941)

One of the most renowned modernist authors of the 20th century, Woolf was an important part of the literary and artistic society of London known as the 'Bloomsbury Set'. Her innovative 'stream of consciousness' technique took her readers in depth into her characters' interior lives in a fast-changing world transformed by new technological advances and shifting gender roles. Woolf's *A Room of One's Own* (1929) is often heralded as a driving force behind the women's literary movement. The long-form feminist essay explores gender inequalities, including the influence of social expectations of women as domestic childbearers. Woolf uses the hypothetical example of Judith Shakespeare, the gifted but uneducated sister of William Shakespeare, who was 'as adventurous, as imaginative, as agog to see the world as he was. But she was not sent to school.' Woolf argues that centuries of prejudice and financial and educational disadvantages deprive women like Judith Shakespeare of the opportunity to develop their creativity. Celebrating women writers such as Jane Austen, the Brontë sisters and George Eliot, she famously argues that a woman requires money and a room of her own in order to write. Woolf experienced the death of her mother, father and brother, and suffered from manic depression for most of her life, tragically committing suicide in 1941.

Virginia Woolf.

The beloved feminist icon: Toni Morrison (1931–2019)

Morrison remains one of the world's most celebrated authors and the first African American woman – and one of the few women – to win the Nobel Prize for Literature, in 1993. Born Chloe Ardelia Wofford, Morrison grew up in Ohio when racial violence was pervasive. When she was only two years old, her family's landlord set their apartment building on fire with the family inside because they could not afford the rent. She was an avid reader and, encouraged by her parents, poured her energy into her studies, graduating from the prestigious Historically Black University,

Toni Morrison.

Nawal el Saadawi.

Howard University and then Cornell University with a graduate degree in American Literature. She was the first Black female fiction editor at Random House Press in New York City.

Her critically acclaimed writing explores Black identity in America, and especially the extreme discrimination experienced by Black women. Her first novel, *The Bluest Eye* (1970), made waves in the American literary landscape for its unflinching portrayal of the experience of a young Black girl in an America where beauty, sexuality, human value and race are starkly interconnected. The novel tells the story of a young African American girl, Pecola Breedlove, who tries to escape from the emotional abuse of her family and classmates by dreaming that she will one day have blue eyes, like the movie star Shirley Temple (though in fact Temple's eyes were dark brown and were recoloured to be blue in some illustrations). The book's penetrating exploration of racism and child molestation resulted in many attempts to ban it from American schools and libraries.

Morrison's later novels, including *Sula* (1973), *Song of Solomon* (1977) and *Beloved* (1987), also delve into the lives of African American women and men dealing with the traumatic legacies of slavery in the 19th and 20th centuries. Along with 11 novels, Morrison wrote plays and children's books. Her work has been made into films, opera and songs, and she was professor of humanities at Princeton University. She earned countless prestigious awards throughout her lifetime, including the Pulitzer Prize and Presidential Medal of Freedom from President Barack Obama.

The feminist firebrand: Nawal el Saadawi (1931–2021)

The Egyptian author, activist and physician Nawal El Saadawi was an emblem of women's rights movements in the Middle East. She experienced female circumcision at a very young age and rebelled against her family's attempts to marry her at the age of 10. She was able to access a school education, where she excelled, and graduated from the University of Cairo with a scholarship to study medicine. As a renowned doctor and then director general for public health education, she published *Women and Sex* (1972). The book was the first in a series that protested against violent control of women's bodies, from female genital mutilation that reduces a woman's sexual pleasure to rituals fixated on preserving a young girl's virginity for her husband. Soon afterwards, she lost her high-ranking job, the health magazine she founded was shut down, and *Women and Sex* was banned in Egypt.

Despite this, El Saadawi continued writing fiction focused on gender issues, including *Woman at Point Zero* (1975), which examines how childhood and marital abuse leads to prostitution, and *Love in the Kingdom of Oil* (1993), which uses a dreamscape narrative to delve into a world where husband and boss are interchangeably experienced by women, and female self-determination is incomprehensible for men. Her most influential book, *The Hidden Face of Eve* (1977), pushes back on Western feminism, positing that patriarchy and poverty – not Islam – oppress Arab women. She argued that 'women are pushed to be just bodies, either to be veiled under religion or to be veiled by makeup. They are taught that they shouldn't face the world with their real face.' In 1981, under President Anwar el-Sadat, El Saadawi was jailed for six months as an enemy of the state for her outspoken political views, during which time she wrote *Memoirs from the Women's Prison* (1983) using an eyebrow pencil on a roll of toilet paper.

After she was released, El Saadawi founded the Arab Women's Solidarity Association (AWSA), where she combined feminism with pan-Arabism. She continued as a powerful voice for change, including visiting Greenham Common in Berkshire in the 1980s and campaigning against the Gulf War in the 1990s. El Saadawi left Egypt in 1993 after threats to her life, teaching at Duke University in North Carolina before returning to Egypt in 1996. She continued her activism, participating in the anti-Mubarak protests of the Arab Spring in Tahrir Square in 2011. In 2018, when asked about toning down her criticism, she responded, 'I should be more aggressive, because the world is becoming more aggressive and we need people to speak loudly against injustices.'

The prophet of dystopia: Margaret Atwood (b. 1939)

The Canadian author Margaret Atwood (b. 1939) is globally acclaimed for her fiction writing of future dystopias governed by patriarchal and discriminatory practices. Atwood initially came to public attention as a poet in the 1960s, when she focused on human alienation from one another and the natural world. In her first novel, *The Edible Woman* (1979) – described by Atwood as a proto-feminist novel – the female protagonist, Marian, finds that her consumer- and male-dominated world disengages her body from her very self. Food, for Marian, symbolizes that struggle and eventual rebellion against it.

Margaret Atwood.

The handmaid modesty costumes of crimson cloaks and white bonnets have been used by women's rights demonstrators around the world as a powerful symbol to protest against the oppression of women and control over their bodies. The costume has been adopted by pro-choice protesters in Ireland's successful referendum and abortion rights campaigners in Argentina. At the 2017 Women's March, signs read 'Make Margaret Atwood fiction again'.

Atwood's most acclaimed novel is *The Handmaid's Tale* (1985) and its sequel, *The Testaments* (2019). The book is constructed as a written record of a woman living in a terrifying patriarchal, white-supremacist future state known as the Republic of Gilead. The society's population is shrinking from a toxic environment where the ability to have children is greatly reduced. The central character, Offred, is one of a group of 'handmaids', forcibly mandated to produce children for the ruling class of men, the 'commanders'. The novel examines themes surrounding the subjugation of women in a patriarchal society, the suppression of female reproductive rights and the ways in which women resist attempts to deprive them of agency and individuality. It has since been made into a film, opera, ballet, graphic novel and TV series, the latter of which was co-produced by Atwood and won 11 Emmys.

Atwood is best known as a feminist writer in that she focuses on the complexities of female experiences, but she is also an environmental activist. Her speculative fiction novels such as the *MaddAddam Trilogy* (2003, 2009, 2013) and *The Handmaid's Tale* centre on unhabitable toxic wastelands caused by human activity and neglect. In describing potential futures, Atwood also explores hopeful change, writing that her dystopian worlds are 'the yellow brick road we see before us, unless we change our wicked ways'.

The Chicana feminist champion: Sandra Cisneros (b. 1954)

Since publishing her iconic first novel *The House on Mango Street* (1983), Sandra Cisneros (b. 1954) has been a powerful voice in literature and a pioneer for Chicano (Mexican American) writers. Chicano literature focuses on the dual cultural experiences of people of Mexican descent. US annexation from 1845 forced Mexico to cede over half its territory, which became the US southwest. Over time, Chicanos developed a distinct culture at the interstices of Mexican and American cultural spheres. Chicano culture, expressed through literature and other cultural practices, has been continuously shaped by Mexican migration to the USA across subsequent decades.

Sandra Cisneros.

Cisneros is a major contributor to Chicano literature, experimenting with literary styles that speak to her own experiences growing up with a culturally hybrid identity and in a context of economic inequality. *The House on Mango Street* is a modern classic of Chicano literature that is based partly on Cisneros's own experiences. Organized as a collection of vignettes, it follows a year in the life of Esperanza Cordero, a young Chicana girl growing up in Chicago's Hispanic district. The novel deals with challenging subjects of domestic violence, racism and sexual harassment as Esperanza faces the realities of living as a young woman in a poor, patriarchal and marginalized community.

Cisneros continues to bring the experiences of Chicana women to the fore in later works such as *Woman Hollering Creek and Other Stories* (1991). In this collection of short stories and vignettes, she focuses on the duality of Mexican and American culture in the lives of Chicano children through a variety of narrative techniques. She explores not only adolescence in an oppressive society but also subjects such as race relations and sexuality, including experiences of being a gay Chicano. Along with Chicana writers such as Gloria Anzaldúa and Cherríe Moraga, Cisneros fills a void by addressing the marginalization of cultural minorities and gender inequality in patriarchal American and Mexican cultures.

The voice of nonconformity: Sayaka Murata (b. 1979)

The Japanese author Sayaka Murata (b. 1979) has achieved global renown for her exploration of social nonconformity when it comes to sex, gender roles and reproduction. For close to 18 years, Murata worked in convenience stores in Japan, where she made close observations of everyday life. In her best-selling novel *Convenience Store Woman* (2016), which won Japan's prestigious Akutagawa Prize and was the first of her novels to be translated into English, she focuses on the life of Keiko Furukura. Keiko is a 36-year-old woman who is uninterested in progressing from her part-time job at the Hiiromachi Station Smile Mart. Keiko, like other characters in Murata's stories, is indifferent to dating and prefers asexual relationships. She defies the homogenizing pressures of social expectations in Japan of marrying and having a traditionally 'successful' career.

The theme of asexuality and nonconformity to social standards also structures Murata's novel *Earthlings* (2020). Her female protagonist, Natsuki, is also indifferent to the 'rules of life' of pursuing a career and 'manufacturing children'. Together with an asexual man she meets online, also averse to sex or romance, Natsuki becomes convinced she is an alien and all humans are brainwashed workers in a baby-making factory.

Murata's writing captures changing but still conflicting social standards in Japan. More than two-thirds of women in Japan now work and the majority are highly educated, but women still only make up a small percentage of top managerial and political positions. In *The Birth Murder* (2014), Murata depicts a future society where women are provided with a contraceptive implant from puberty, sex is an act of lust and pregnancy occurs through assisted fertilization in which men are given artificial uteruses. Murata challenges the belief that the reproductive body is exclusive to women, as well as questioning concepts of pregnancy and motherhood. Like Atwood, Murata uses surrealist worlds to push her readers to think differently about what is 'normal' or 'right'. She writes in a trademark deadpan style that makes potentially fantastical ideas seem mundane.

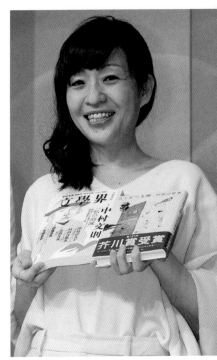

Sayaka Murata with her prize-winning novel Kombini Ningen (Convenience Store Woman) *in 2016.*

SLOWLY CHANGING GLOBAL RECOGNITION

The Nobel Prize in Literature is the highest international award bestowed on an individual for their writing. Yet, despite the brilliance of women writers across history, it has taken years for women to be internationally recognized. Since its inception in 1901, only 16 women had been awarded the Nobel Literature Prize as of 2021 (13.6 per cent of 118 awarded), starting with the Swedish author Selma Lagerlöf (1858–1940) in 1909. In 2018, the prestigious literary prize was cancelled owing to convictions of sexual misconduct and financial malpractice against one of the Academy members (known as 'The Eighteen'), the body that chooses the laureates for the prize. Since then, the Swedish Academy has announcement a commitment to gender equality and a move away from a Eurocentric, male-oriented focus. From 2019, at least one-third of the chairs will belong to female Academy members.

Selma Lagerlöf was the first woman to win the Nobel Prize in Literature and the first woman to be admitted as a lifelong member to the Swedish Academy. She set her captivating novels, such as Gösta Berling's Saga (1891) *and* The Wonderful Adventures of Nils (1904), *in haunting landscapes rooted in Swedish folktales, breaking from the realism of the time.*

We should all be feminists

Chapter 7

WE SHOULD ALL BE FEMINISTS

For many, the word 'feminism' holds negative connotations. It has been misconstrued as vilifying men or stripping them of opportunities. The award-winning Nigerian author Chimamanda Ngozi Adichie (b. 1977) has pushed back against these stigmas. She famously gave a 2012 TEDx talk in London in which she discussed what it means to be a feminist. In her talk, and later book of the same name, *We Should All Be Feminists* (2014), Adichie advances a powerful definition of 21st-century feminism grounded in understanding and inclusion. Feminism, Adichie points out, is not an insult, but a commitment to egalitarianism that should be embraced by everyone. It is not about reversing gender roles and making men inferior, but about creating equal opportunities for everyone. Being a feminist involves challenging cultural and social restrictions that limit people's ability to become who they want to be. This vision of a feminist world emphasizes true inclusivity and centres the experiences of historically marginalized groups, including people of colour and with disabilities, and non-binary and trans individuals. Rather than a gender-blind or colour-blind stance, an intersectional approach is crucial in ensuring one another's capacity to flourish.

We have seen feminists successfully fight for voting rights, more egalitarian workplaces, safer public spaces and reproductive rights. So, what does a feminist future look like today?

What do you picture when you think about the future?

The future involves both looking backwards and being inspired by people's creative energies, but it is also a case of imagining where we might progress to. Intersectional feminism foregrounds futurist visions with concerns of social and racial justice and economic equity. Feminism is intersectional when it focuses on the impacts on those with the least privilege and resources. Intersectionality requires recognizing historical disadvantages and fighting for structural change for the future. This can involve supporting movements from disability rights to labour activism.

Afrofuturist feminism

The subgenre of science fiction is well known for utopian themes. Authors experiment with different speculative visions around what the future could look like. The 'Afrofuturism' movement emerged in the 1970s but gained traction as a named genre from the 1990s. Through the creative arts, Black artists tell stories of their restricted pasts together with their complex presents to envisage a different, and often more hopeful, future. From literature to film to music and the visual arts, Afrofuturist creations are about harnessing the transformative power of art and African cultural forms to imagine and advance change. Works of Afrofuturism often feature science and technological innovations as seen through a Black lens.

The Kingdom of Wakanda is a fictional East African country in the Marvel comic and film Black Panther. Wakanda is technologically advanced and free from European colonialism. The country is protected by the Dora Milaje, a team of women who are some of the best fighters in the world.

The problem with gender is that it prescribes how we should be rather than recognizing how we are.
– Chimamanda Ngozi Adichie

Octavia Butler.

Nalo Hopkinson.

Octavia Butler

Since the 1990s, Afrofuturism has been dominated by women. The African American science fiction author Octavia Butler (1947–2006) was at the vanguard of Afrofuturism. From the 1970s, Butler's work brought new perspectives to the white, male-dominated science fiction genre. In her essay 'Positive Obsession', Butler emphasized the ability of speculative fiction to kick-start progressive political change. Many of Butler's novels feature powerful Black female protagonists finding societal solutions to apocalyptic events. Her stories feature multi-ethnic communities of African, European, LatinX and Asian descent, as well as extraterrestrials, different species (including vampires) and cross-species. This hybridity allows for flexible understandings of gender and sexuality and offers futurist solutions that revolve around co-operation and egalitarianism.

Nalo Hopkinson

A succession of Black female science fiction authors has followed Butler, including Nalo Hopkinson (b. 1960), Nnedi Okorafor (b. 1974), Karen Lord (b. 1968) and N.K. Jemisin (b. 1972). Jemisin was the first Black female writer to win the prestigious Hugo Award for best novel, going on to win it three years in a row: the only writer to ever do so. Her Broken Earth trilogy is set on a huge continent known as the Stillness, in a far-future Earth plagued with massive disasters called Seasons. The population is very diverse and there are no racial or gendered hierarchies. Women, men, queer and trans people are in leadership in equal numbers. None is considered weak or unsuitable for certain jobs. In many cases, the gender variance between people's bodies is not that different and gender identity is open for personal interpretation. However, the Stillness has its own societal divisions. Among humanity's survivors are 'orogenes': a small minority of the population born with ability to control the Earth's energy. They become targets and experience extreme systematic oppression. In her writing, Jemison points to the arbitrariness of societal divisions and the need to upend sexist and racist status quos.

JANELLE MONAE AND CINDI MAYWEATHER

The American singer and actress Janelle Monáe (b. 1985) has built her music around a science fiction universe. She adopted the alter ego of Cindi Mayweather, an android on the run from Metropolis, a dystopian slave droid-powered city. Monáe reclaims sci-fi tropes advanced by white male writers of the 20th century, mapping them on to her own identity. She has used the android metaphor to imagine queer Afrofuturist visions, where oppressions can be defeated by reclaiming your inner power.

Ecofeminism – a philosophy that combines environmental and feminist concerns. Both are deeply impacted by patriarchal domination. In many societies, nature and women have long been viewed as 'other', particularly in those where fossil fuel industrialism has been rampant.

Ecofeminism

Climate change is having a catastrophic effect on regions around the world. Greenhouse gas emissions generated by burning non-renewable fossil fuels such as coal, oil and natural gas have made global warming over the next decades inevitable. This leads to dramatic weather events including more frequent and severe heat waves, droughts, storms, rising sea levels and warming oceans. As climate change worsens, weather events directly harm plant and animal habitats, and affect people's livelihoods and communities.

But while climate change is a collective problem, the impacts are disproportionately experienced by marginalized groups, including women. Globally, women experience higher rates of poverty from the pressures of differential roles and responsibilities. In many countries, women are responsible for the majority of agricultural work and food production. This increases their economic and personal vulnerability when harvests are lost from temperature rise, droughts and floods. Women also have disproportionate primary-care responsibilities for children, families and communities. As resources become scare, this usually unpaid care work increases. Women also have less access to decision-making structures, technology and training that would make them more adaptable to the impacts of climate change. Ecofeminism focuses on the reality that climate change is a 'threat multiplier' that harms the poor, women, disabled, queer and trans people, particularly those of colour, the most. Marginalized communities also experience more environmental challenges, including issues around air pollution and unsanitary water. Ecofeminists take an intersectional approach to support higher-risk populations.

Ecofeminism took off from heavily associating women with nature. Critics charged that arguing women have an intrinsic connection with nature enforces the very binary that feminism should try to break. Instead, the non-essentialist view argues that women along with nature cannot be stereotyped, but that there are connections between class, race, gender and species domination.

We hold the future of the Earth in our hands.

Ecofeminists have made huge stride in recent years. Now, many climate justice leaders are women, people of colour, queer and indigenous. There is an increased diversity of representation across key government roles and leadership positions, including when it comes to enacting major environmental policy changes. This kind of intersectional environmentalism is important: those who have had experiences with institutional sexism and other inequalities often understand where change is needed the most.

THE CHIPKO MOVEMENT

This was an Indian forest conservation movement that began in the 1970s in the Himalayan region of Uttarakhand. Support for the movement came primarily from the mass participation of female villagers. Women are crucial to Uttarakhand's agrarian economy and so directly related to environmental degradation and deforestation, which resulted in reduced agricultural yields, firewood and water for drinking. Chipko inspired ecofeminist groups and environmental movements around the world.

Rachel Carson

The American conservationist Rachel Carson (1907–64) was a major figure of contemporary environmental movements. Her influential book *Silent Spring* (1962) was a landmark work of ecological journalism. Carson powerfully warned about the dangers of pesticides on world ecosystems. As a result of her awareness-raising, the USA banned substances such as dichlorodiphenyltrichloroethane (DDT) and created the United States Environmental Protection Agency.

Rachel Carson.

Vandana Shiva.

Vandana Shiva

Vandana Shiva (b. 1952) is an Indian ecologist and environmental activist, often referred to as 'Gandhi of grain' for her work in the anti-GMO (genetically modified organisms) movement. Shiva was also heavily involved in the Chipko movement. In her advocacy, she draws on the knowledge of indigenous people in pushing for local, biodiverse chemical-free food systems.

The future of feminism is being advanced by those on the front lines of environmental activism.

The next generation of organizers is working to combat climate change and advance radically new visions for the future of society.

Greta Thunberg

The Swedish youth climate activist Greta Thunberg (b. 2003) has drawn the attention of global leaders to climate change and demanded immediate action. She became well known after her school strike protests outside the Swedish parliament, where she pressured the government to meet carbon emissions targets. Her campaign went global and inspired young people around the world to organize their own strikes under the 'Fridays for Future' movement. For her famous speech at the 2019 UN Climate Action Summit, Thunberg sailed across the Atlantic to New York City to avoid carbon-intensive flying. She told world leaders they were not doing enough, saying, 'You all come to us young people for hope. How dare you? You have stolen my dreams and my childhood with your empty words.'

Greta Thunberg.

Xiye Bastida.

Xiye Bastida

Xiye Bastida (b. 2002) is a Mexican-Chilean climate activist and member of the Indigenous Mexican Otomi-Toltec people. She is a leading advocate for indigenous and immigrant inclusion in climate activism. In her advocacy, she has flagged up patterns of environmental racism where poor countries in the Global South and Black and brown neighbourhoods in the Global North bear the brunt of toxic pollution. Bastida is a co-founder of Re-Earth Initiative, which focuses on inclusivity and intersectionality, including the importance of intergenerational collaboration and solidarity.

Isra Hirsi

Isra Hirsi (b. 2003) is an American environmental justice and Black Lives Matter organizer. She co-founded the US Youth Climate Strike in 2019 and has organized hundreds of thousands of young people to strike for climate justice. Hirsi is the daughter of Somali-American congresswoman Ilhan Omar, a member of the group of Democratic politicians known as 'the Squad'. They have pushed for progressive changes such as public healthcare and the Green New Deal, which focuses on weaning the USA off fossil fuels and planet-warming greenhouse gas emission, as well as providing high-paying jobs in clean-energy sectors. Hirsi brings these politics to young people, including voicing her experiences as a young Black Muslim woman, to encourage diversity in the climate movement.

ABOVE:
Isra Hirst.

RIGHT:
Pınar Sinopoulos-Lloyd.

Pınar Sinopoulos-Lloyd

Pınar Sinopoulos-Lloyd is a non-binary, queer person of colour who co-founded Queer Nature, a Colorado-based nature education and ancestral skills programme for the LGBTQ+ community and its allies. For non-binary and trans people, there is often minimal cultural access to outdoor recreation. Boy scouts, girl scouts and wilderness skills groups frequently operate on a binary basis and infuse a colonial mentality of conquering and competition, rather than inclusive relationships with the land. Queer Nature merges values of conservation and environmental justice with an inclusive form of environmentalism that advocates for the protection of all people and the planet. Sinopolous-Lloyd asks: what might a decolonially-informed queer ancestral futurism look like?

Isatou Ceesay, photographed in front of a pile of discarded rag from the clothing industry.

Isatou Ceesay

Isatou Ceesay (b. 1972) is a Gambian social entrepreneur and activist who is known as the 'Queen of Recycling'. Few parts of the Gambia receive a municipal waste collection service. Even though they are often given out freely, plastic bags have devastating health and environmental implications: plastic bags block drains, which leads to disease, and the burning of plastic waste is incredibly toxic. In response, in 1997 Ceesay co-founded the community-driven Recycling Centre of N'Jau in North Gambia. Initially, the project's goal was to help people understand the importance of recycling plastic waste: a material that accounts for 20 per cent of waste in the Gambia. Gradually, the project grew into the N'Jau Recycling and Income Generation Group, a revolutionary grassroots recycling scheme that provides women with income-generating opportunities. Members collect waste materials themselves and help recycle it into sellable products including bags, mats, purses and jewellery. There is also home-composting training to help communities produce their own high-quality organic fertilizer. Through this project and her wider recycling movement, Ceesay works with more than 11,000 people across the Gambia, providing livelihoods for women in particular and improving the environment.

FEMALE SEED GUARDIANS

Women have come together around the world to mitigate the effects of climate change through grassroots efforts. In many countries, women are sharing traditional ecological knowledge and collaborating on seed-banking initiatives. Seeds are essential to agriculture, but organic seeds are hard to source. The market is filled with genetically modified and hybrid seeds, which often cannot be replanted and come at significant costs.

Vanastree is one example of a women's seed-saving collective in western India. Through the project, women home gardeners and farmers exchange ideas about flood-resistant indigenous seeds to tackle the effects of climate change. Vanastree maintains an open-source seed collection and focuses on cultivating the entire region as a seed storehouse for public

use, while also building the capacity of rural women leaders and advocating for the rights of female farmers. This is significant, given that according to Oxfam, nearly 75 per cent of full-time agricultural workers in India are women, with female farmers producing as much as 80 per cent of India's food.

The feminism of our future

Although it might seem logical, the opposite of male-centred politics – and feminism's future – is not flipping the tables to a female domination of politics and power hierarchies. Rather, it is moving beyond a zero-sum game to a collective and inclusive sharing of power. The journalist and magazine editor Ann Friedman (b. 1982) and businesswoman and writer Aminatou Sow (b. 1985) describe this best using the term 'shine theory'. This theory of power is based on the idea that 'I don't shine if you don't shine'. It advocates for lifting one another up, rather than reducing one another's glow.

This future feminism advances a world where all people are supported to achieve their full potential. It focuses on a world in which all workers are valued for their economic contributions and where professional women who work outside of their homes do not advance power using the precarious labour of domestic workers in their homes. The COVID-19 pandemic brought many of these stark inequalities to light. It magnified people's unequal access to healthcare, safe housing, education, employment, food, care and protection. It showed how the work of maintaining a home and caring for children falls disproportionately to women, even when they have full-time jobs and pay for help. Even more than this, people who are paid to work in domestic labour or care work, such as house cleaning, home healthcare services or elder care, are generally poorly compensated and denied basic workplace protections and benefits. These jobs are predominately done by migrants and women of colour. By laying bare these structural inequalities, crises such as the pandemic are crucial moments of reset for rebuilding societies.

An inclusive feminist movement is grounded in the lived experiences of Native, Black, LatinX and Asian women, of queer, lesbian and trans women, poor women, sex workers and women with disabilities. This movement centres on a politics of liberation and belonging, including foregrounding the intersectional concerns of those who have long been marginalized from mainstream feminism. It focuses on adding value to each other and valuing one another's lives and contributions with respect. Identity politics will be normalized so that being a feminist, a person of colour, queer and progressive will not be exceptional or symptomatic of marginalization. Our future feminism will be a feminism of political leaders and presidents, of scientists, artists and innovators, and of social justice leaders and intellectuals. A feminism that is inclusive and intersectional benefits everyone, including women, men and those who are gender non-conforming. The next wave of feminism is on the horizon and is one in which we can all be a part!

Women and young girl protesting for equal pay at the Change the Rules workers' union rally in central Melbourne on 23 October 2018 wear outfits and strike poses referencing Rosie the Riveter.

Further reading

Abu-Lughod, Lila. 2013. *Do Muslim Women Need Saving?* Cambridge: Harvard University Press.

Adichie, Chimamanda Ngozi. 2014. *We Should All Be Feminists.*

Adovasio, J.M., Olga Soffer, and Jake Page. 2016. *The Invisible Sex: Uncovering the True Roles of Women in Prehistory.* London: Routledge.

de Beauvoir, Simone. 2009. *The Second Sex.* Translated by Constance Borde and Sheila Malovany-Chevalier. London: Vintage Books.

Butler, Judith. 1990. *Gender Trouble.* Abingdon: Routledge.

Collins, Patricia Hill. 2014. *Black Feminist Thought: Knowledge, Consciousness and the Politics of Empowerment.* London: Routledge.

Dark Star, eds. 2012. *Quiet Rumours: An Anarcha-Feminist Reader.* Oakland: AK Press.

Davis, Angela. 2019. *Women, Race & Class.* London: Penguin Books.

Duran, Lucy. 1995. 'Birds of Wasulu: Freedom of Expression and Expressions of Freedom in the Popular Music of Southern Mali.' *British Journal of Ethnomusicology* (4): 101-134.

Hall, Kim K. and Ásta, eds. 2021. *The Oxford Handbook of Feminist Philosophy.* Oxford: Oxford University Press.

hooks, bell. 2015. *Feminism is for Everybody.* New York: Routledge.

Joyce, Rosemary. 2008. *Ancient Bodies, Ancient Lives.* New York: Thames and Hudson.

Kendall, Mikki. 2020. *Hood Feminism: Notes From the Women That A Movement Forgot.* London: Bloosmbury Publishing.

Lourde, Audre. 2019. *Sister Outsider.* London: Penguin Books.

Lynn Budin, Stephanie and Jean Macintosh Turfa. 2016. *Women in Antiquity: Real Women Across the Ancient World.* London: Routlege.

Mies, Maria and Vandana Shiva. 2014. *Ecofeminism.* London: Zed Books.

Plath, Sylvia. 2008. *The Bell Jar.* London: Faber & Faber.

Talpade Mohanty, Chandra. 2003. *Feminism without Borders: Decolonizing Theory, Practicing Solidarity.* Durham: Duke University Press.

Walker, Alice. 1984. *In Search of Our Mothers' Gardens: Womanist Prose.* San Diego: Harcourt Brace Jovanovich.

Woolf, Virginia. 1967. *A Room of One's Own.* New Delhi: Prabhat Prakashan.

Index

Picture credits

ABC News/Emily Butcher 151; **AFP** 103 below left; **Afterall Journal** 201; **Alamy** 11 left, 14 top left, 15 below, 25 left, 28 left, 33 left, 35 right, 49 top, 61 left, 65 below, 80 below, 81 top, 85, 90, 100 below, 172 top, 175 left, 177 top, 188 top, 190 top, 192, 195, 196 below, 197 top, 199 below, 210, 211 right, 215 top, 216 below, 242, 141 below; **Aline Rakotoson Babelon,** 212 below right, **Amber Fares** 229 below; **Andrew Berry Courtesy the artist and Lehmann Maupin, New York, Hong Kong, Seoul, and London** 217 top, **AP Photo/Susan Walsh** 150 top, **Associated Press** 188 below; **Bibliotheque Nationale de France** 61 right; **BJJ Eastern Europe** 227 below; **Bowery Boys History** 181 top left; **Diego Riviera and Frida Kahlo Archives, Banco de México, Fiduciary of the Trust of the Diego Riviera and Frida Kahlo** 211 left; **Erhabor Emokpae** 78; **Getty Images** 6, 8, 15 top, 17, 49 below, 74 below, 81 below, 87, 95 below, 100 top, 104, 107 below, 108 below, 110 below, 117 top, 123 top right, 124 below, 125 top, 128, 131 below, 136, 138 top, 138 below left, 141 top, 145 below, 146 top, 146 below left, 149 top, 149 below, 152, 153 below, 153 top, 155, 156, 158 top, 162 left, 165 top, 169, 170 right, 171, 172 below, 175 right, 181 below, 187 below, 190 below, 194, 197 below, 199 top, 200, 207, 208 below right, 212 top right, 212 below left, 214 left, 216 top, 221 top, 222 top, 222 below, 223 below, 226, 228 top, 228 below, 235 below, 238, 239 top, 243 top, 243 below, 246 below, 247 top, 247 below, 248 top, 204, **Guardian NG** 95 top, **Guatemala MUNAE** 45 top right, **Harmonia Rosales** 20, **Achalugoart.wordpress.com** 83 right, **Imgrum** 80 top, **InSight Australia** 97 top, **Jim Lo Scalzo/EPA** 117 below, **JuJu Films** 135 below, **Kompasiana** 132 top, Kris Walters/Courtesy of the artist and Roberts Projects, Los Angeles, CA 214 right; **Library of Congress** 93, 94, 99, 108 top, 109 left, 126, 146 below right; **Luca Borghi** 120 top; **Luke Duggleby/Climate Heroes** 249; **Maria Blanco Lora/UNFPA** 158 below; **Metropolitan Museum of Art** 27 below, 29 right, 30, 77, 88; **NARA** 177 below; **NASA** 121 top left, 121 below left; **National Museum Uyo** 133; **Polity.org** 173 below; **Public domain** 205, 225 top, 12 below, 13, 14 top right, 21 top, 21 below, 23, 26, 28 right, 40 top, 51, 52, 56 top, 59, 63 top, 64 right, 64 below left, 71 below, 72 left, 73, 75, 79 below, 89 top, 101 top, 106, 107 centre, 123 below right, 124 top, 129, 130, 134, 135 top, 142 top, 147, 148, 173 top, 178 left, 178 right, 183 top, 183 Centre, 183 below, 184 left, 185, 186, 187 top, 193, 209 top, 231, 233 left, 11 right, 42 left;, **Randall Haas/University of California** 12 top, **RAWA (Revolutionary Association of the Women of Afghanistan)** 157 right, **Riza Fanani Novianto for Liputan6** 132 below, **Robert Graham/Wordpress** 182, **San Antonio Museum of Art** 68 top; **Shutterstock** 10, 22 top, 24 right, 25 right, 36 top, 36 below, 37, 45 below, 48, 56 below, 63 below, 64 top, 67, 68 below, 69 top, 70 top, 70 below, 71 left, 71 right, 72 right, 89 below, 92, 96 left, 96 right, 98 below, 98 top, 101 below, 103 top left, 103 below right, 105, 109 right, 110 top, 111 top, 113 below, 114 below, 115, 116, 159, 160, 162 right, 198 top, 198 below, 202, 223 top, 225 below, 227 top, 235 top, 236, 237, 240, 244 top, 244 below, 245, 250, 251; **Sisterstong** 150 below; **Smithsonian** 142 below, 143 left; **Tai Entertainment** 230 ; **Taproot for Save Our Sisters** 22 below; **Teaching for Change** 168 top left; **US National Park Service** 120 below; **Via Legislative Assembly Costa Rica** 107 top; **Virginia Museum of Fine Art** 23 ; **WeavingEarth** 248 below; Wendy Red Star 217 below; **Whole Family Health** 191 below; **Wikimedia Commons,** 84, 18, 19 top, 19 below, 24 left, 27 top, 29 left, 31, 32 top, 32 below, 33 right, 34 top, 34 below, 35 left, 38 right, 38 left, 39 top, 39 below, 40 below, 41 top, 41 below, 42 right, 43, 44, 45 top left, 46 left, 46 right, 47, 50, 55, 57, 58 left, 58 right, 60 below, 60 top, 62, 65 top, 66 top, 66 below, 69 below, 76, 79 top, 82, 86 top, 86 below, 97 below, 102 left, 102 right, 111 below, 112 left, 112 right, 113 top, 114 top, 118, 119 top, 119 below, 121 top right, 121 below right, 122, 123 top left, 125 below right, 125 below left, 131 top, 137, 138 below right, 139 top, 139 below, 144 right, 144 left, 145 right, 154 top, 157, 164 left, 165 below, 166 below, 166 right, 170 left, 176 left, 179, 180, 180 top, 184 below, 189 right, 191, 196 top, 206 top, 206 below right, 206 top left, 206 top right, 208 below left, 208 left, 209 top, 213 below, 215, 218 below, 218 left, 219 right, 220, 220 top, 221 below, 224 below, 229, 232 top, 232 below, 233 top, 234 right, 239, 246 below, 246 top; **Yagazieemezi.com** 83 left; **YouTube** 74 top.